SEO

Search Engine Optimization

MADE SIMPLE FOR 2011

Jason McCormick

Royal House Publishing

Beverly Hills, CA

Presents:

SEO Made Simple

For 2011

Jason McCormick

SEO/SEM Expert

Royal House Publishing

SEO Made Simple For 2011

The material contained in this book are not sponsored by, endorsed by, or affiliated with Microsoft Corporation, Google.com, Bing.com, Yahoo!, MSN, Live, or any other search engine and/or products, code, or software shown herein. All logos are trademarks of their respective owners.

ISBN-13: 978-0615426723 (Royal House Publishing Inc.)

ISBN-10: 0615426727

Royal House Publishing has attempted whenever possible throughout this book to distinguish proprietary trademarks from descriptive terms by following capitalization and style used by their respective owners.

Images licensed for print from Fotolia US.

This book is dedicated to:

This book is dedicated to all of my clients at WebSEOPros.com who have had faith in me to get their businesses where they wanted to be on the Internet.

About the author – Jason McCormick

Jason McCormick (Jason@WebSEOPros.com), is well known in the Search Engine Optimization (SEO) industry. Some of his techniques have been learned and put in to use by many others through books and news articles he has written. Before being an SEO professional, Jason worked as a developer and was one of the founding fathers of the algorithms used in many of today's largest search engines. He regularly consults with other SEO companies in need of information on what has changed with search engine algorithms.

One of his major accomplishments, Jason along with other developers has designed a custom made reporting system for his clients which allows bots, crawlers, and spiders to scan the Internet on a weekly basis for keyword ranking changes, competition optimization changes, mentions of customers names or domains in social media as well as blogs, keyword rankings on all the major search engines, detect optimization issues, and it can also detect design problems and changes immediately on his clients web sites.

The system allows every customer to receive a weekly updated real-time report to his customers.

Acknowledgements

I need to thank my family for all that they do to support me in my endeavors. Also I need to thank all the people at Royal House Publishing and all the dozens of people who endured sleepless nights to make this dream a reality.

Table Of Contents

8

Introduction

Nothing is more certain in the world of Search Engine Optimization (SEO) than the absolute certainty that requirements for the major search engines will change over time. Rankings, indexing techniques, search traffic, search engine algorithms, your website's structure and the content are all variables that can help you or hinder your websites viability.

Ten years ago I was on the other side of the fence. I was working for what is now the third largest search engine. I was tasked with developing the algorithms and techniques which are still used in all the major search engines. Today, I manage some of the most profitable websites on the Internet.

When I take over a website to do professional SEO services, I give my new clients a guarantee. The guarantee is that in 6 months I will have paid for myself many times over in the returns they get from my services. The reason for this? I know what I am doing and in the past 6 years I have never seen an SEO company which I couldn't outperform or a competitive keyword I couldn't take on for my customer.

Google, by its own admission, makes on average one or more changes to its search algorithm every single day. It is difficult to identify most of these changes, let alone know precisely when they occurred. On occasion the search engines themselves acknowledge a change to their ranking algorithm or indexing system such as the addition of "Google Caffeine", which is a new indexing system we will talk about later in this book.

There are many other changes in the search engine environment that are both evident to users, and typically confirmed by the search engines. These can include changes to the layout of search result pages, inclusion of new verticals or other visual modifications to the search results. So even though I am writing this book to teach you the current techniques, if you are a company who relies on the Internet and your company website as its core source of income I would tell you right now. Stop reading and get a professional company to provide your SEO services. Of course I recommend my company of course. But there are more scam artists than there are SEO's that really know what they are doing. The following is a list of SEO companies I would recommend that know what they are doing and are reasonable priced for the job they do:

- SEODEO (www.SEODEO.com)
- Website SEO Zone (www.WebSEOZone.com)
- SEO Technology Masters (SEOTechMasters.com)
- TopRankedListing.com

Since you bought this book you are probably acutely aware that a majority of the planet now turns to the Internet for just about anything they need. Most people are not even accepting the phone books they used to value so much. Not so much as it is a useless tool, but more so because people have a "going green" mindset.

In general, most businesses have to be successful on the Internet in 2011 to survive. To be a successful business on the Internet your web site must display in the search results on page 1 or 2 of a Google, Bing, or Yahoo! search to survive for the focused words people are using to search for the product or services your company provides. Or your business will be a forgotten memory unless you intend to pay for Pay-Per-Clicks which will cost you many times what you are paying to get good SEO service.

Getting to the top of the search results for any given set of search terms has been my job for over 10 years. Now over 250 businesses both large and small have turned to me for advice to become more successful on the Internet.

When I first started in this business, good Meta tagging, a good matching description, and a matching title, is all it took. In 2011 it's not quite that easy. Not only that, now a Meta tag is merely a nice object to have and only one of about 150 different on-page, off-page, and mechanical items you need to worry about every month to get your site optimized and your search engine rankings the best they can be for key search terms you need to be relevant for.

In this book, I am not going to bore you with a super long history of the Internet, or of the history of this person who started this, or for the most part outline algorithms and math equations that each search engine uses.

What I am putting in this book are the facts. Just what you really need to know about Search Engine Optimization (SEO), Social Media Optimization (SMO) and I am doing it in a way that is absolutely easy to understand, right to the point, and in a step-by-step format.

There are a few times I will repeat myself in this book. Particularly items found in the Meta tagging sections found in Chapter 2. I have learned over time that if I don't repeat some of the more important things, people tend to forget and may not get a clear understanding of where items fit in the bigger picture.

This book has a lot to digest and it goes in chronological order so don't miss any chapter of this book and read it in order. I go in steps, just as if I were to take a new web site from a customer and optimize it.

It takes a lot of work, training, and time to keep pace with the latest information and to master every part of search engine optimization. You have to learn it well enough to make adjustments when a web site won't go up in the rankings because of competition in the industry or you're competing with a number of other SEO companies in the same industry. When you go to a national or international campaign level with high competition keywords it is even worse.

Sometimes it is just easier to have professionals do the work. If you find that you are struggling and can't make it work. Skip my book and call me.

My company is called Website SEO Professionals (www.WebSEOPros.com) and we can help you with everything you have read here. We have taken web sites with a Google ranking of "none" and very quickly got them at the top of every search engines for their keywords.

Chapter 1 - Overview of Search Engine Optimization

Why do I need search engines optimization?

Did you spend thousands of dollars on a web site that looks awesome and flashy but doesn't show up anywhere on a search engine unless you type in the full domain name?   Or maybe you realized as a business owner the you are spending thousands of dollars per month on telephone book advertising that doesn't make the phone ring more than a couple of times per month anymore.

Today, virtually every business in the world has to rely on the Internet to stay in business.   Most business owners got sold on the idea of having a website, and most business owners naively thought, "Gee, I have a website now, people will magically know it exists and come see it. YAY"

Then about three months later, they get discouraged and think the Internet is not working or people must not look for their product or service on the Internet because no one calls or orders something from their website. They have spent all this money and time on a flashy website and are now starting to get scared because as a business owner, not making sales is very scary and discouraging.

This is where the business owner sat at the computer, opened up a search engine and slowly typed, "how to market a website" and pressed enter. Soon he is provided listing after listing and sponsored listings galore about Search Engine Optimization (SEO), Search Engine Marketing (SEM), how to submit your website to the search engines, and more, and more.

If the poor business owner wasn't confused before, after an hour of searching through web site after web site he probably is now. The information overload probably caused you as the business owner to look up items, start to research but then a key term started to emerge. The term SEO.   But what is it?

Well most website owners think that even after they let Google and the other search engines know your website exists, that the search engines will also magically know exactly what your website is about and what products or services you are focused on providing.   The assume that the search engines magically know what key terms people will use to search for your website and send people right to your website.   The cash register will ring, the sales will be hopping, the need for employees to process the orders will be immense and you are on your way to happy days.

Three to six months later you are sitting there with all the extra inventory and people to service your potentially explosive growth but nothing is happening. Why?

Well when you think like a consumer, the consumer types in certain search words to find your product or service. But what are they? And even when you figure it out, how do you tell the search engines what they are? And even if the search engines know what your keyword phrases are that you want them to use to tell potential customers you exist, how do you get your website on the first or second page of the search results where all your best competition is at?

Well I will tell you. It is an exact science called Search Engine Optimization (SEO). If it is done right on your web site, you reap all the sales. If you don't have it, or it is done wrong, well just go outside tonight and look at all the stars in the sky. Pick one star, because that is your website. Just one speck in the middle of billions of others.

A Quick History of the Search Engines

The Internet has actually been around for quite some time in the early 1990's. The Internet search engines in the form that we know today didn't come around until the appearance of a site called Wandex in 1993. Wandex was the first to both index and search the index of pages on web sites. In that same year, Excite started using similar technology, which we call "crawling" or indexing a web site. Bing.com is the latest of the major search engines to enter the Internet realm. Here is a list of the major search engines and when they started:

- Excite, 1993
- Yahoo!, 1994
- Web Crawler, 1994
- Lycos, 1994
- Infoseek, 1995
- AltaVista, 1995
- Inktomi, 1996
- Ask, 1997
- Google, 1997
- MSN Search, 1998
- Bing, 2009

Today's search engines are more sophisticated than ever. If you type a word or phrase into a search box and click the search button, you have to wait only a few seconds to get thousands of results. Most of the time those results take you to web sites that are relevant to what you are searching for. Also, on most of the major search engines you will rarely click on a link that doesn't work.

So how does all this work?

The easy answer is search engines use algorithms to process the billions of pieces of information they have collected about web pages on the Internet. The algorithms are a list of filters and rules used to decide which web sites most closely relate to the search that was made. You then see the results of what the algorithms decided were the best results for your searched words or phrases on the screen.

What you don't know is little programs called bots, crawlers, or spiders have visited virtually every web site on the Internet before your search and collected information of the websites it displays. These little programs collect keywords, phrases and other coding located on every web site, and then stores this information in large databases used by the search engines.

Thoroughly confused yet? Let's give an example. Let' say you go to my web site URL such as http://www.WebSEOPros.com. The funny thing is, what you see (also referred to as content) on the web site that comes up accounts for only about 20 percent of what search engines use to decide what makes a web site the most relevant for your keyword searches.

"I have a good-looking web site, better than my competitor! Why am I at the bottom of web searches and why is my competitor at the top of the searches? I even have more Meta tags than him!"

The answer gets a little complicated. It is probably not what you see on the site. It is what is being done on the backend that you don't see!

Often, what is most relevant is the code that makes up the pages, the density of use of the keywords, as well as the relevancy of links into and out of the page.

There are other factors as well: what sites you are listed on, how long your domain has been in existence, the length of your domain's URL renewal term, as well as all the following which we will explain later in this book:

- Optimized Content
- Social Media Optimization (SMO)
- Strategic Tagging
- Web site Submissions
- Domain registration period
- Keyword Research
- Meta delivery
- Title Tag Optimization
- Robots.txt Optimization
- Site mapping
- HTML Source Code
- Frequently Changed Content
- Image & Hyperlink Optimization
- Social Bookmarking
- Blogs
- Press Release Writing
- Article Submissions
- Video Optimization
- RSS Feeds
- Link Development
- Manual Link Requests to Related Sites
- Local & International Search Engines & Directory Listings
- One-Way Links to your website
- Two-Way Links (Reciprocal Links)
- PPC
- HTML design
- ASP. and other coding such as Java and Flash
- Linked URLs

Sometimes it's worth having a professional help you out. I am a professional at this and I will outline this all for you in a step by step, easy to understand way.

What collects all the web site information for the search engines?

The job of collecting information about web pages is performed by automation using an agent called a *crawler, spider,* or *robot(bot)* which is different depending on the search engine. These agents literally look at every URL on the Internet and collect keywords, links, relevant data and phrases on each page. But before it does, you as the network administrator must allow these agents to look at the content the web site provides.

> **NOTE**: *We will discuss how to allow crawler, spider and robots to collect information on a web site later under Meta tagging in the next chapter.*

These crawlers, spider and bots collect information from not only what a visitor of your web site sees but also from the coding behind the scenes. In fact only about 20-25% of your ranking on the major search engines comes from what the users see. The rest comes from the coding and numerous other items we will discuss later in this book.

Search engines like to keep the algorithms they use as secret as possible to make it fair to everyone. In fact it is rare to find any official explanation describing just how a search engine algorithm processes the data it collects and makes decisions on it. It is known only to a rare few who either work for the search engines, or people like me: the ones who spend their entire lives testing algorithms, putting what we learn into practice on real companies' web sites, and placing those companies in the top ten of any search for their specific trophy words.

> **NOTE**: *We will discuss trophy words later in the book in a chapter called "Keywords."*

Search Engine Query Interfaces

The query interface is the most familiar part of the search engine. This is the little box where you type a few words related to what you want to find and like magic, a list of web sites shows up. It is rare anymore that you find a link to a web site that isn't relevant to your search words or a web site that no longer exists. You also won't find web sites without updated content.

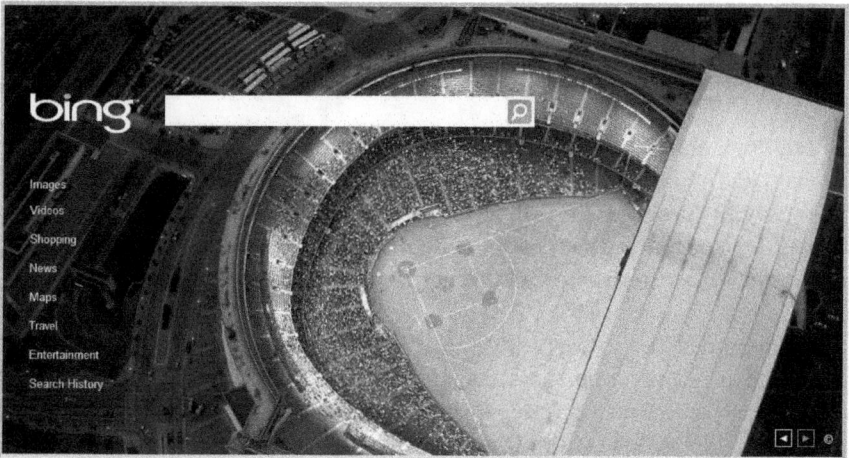

Figure 1.1

The Bing.com search interface is shown in Figure 1.1. This is Microsoft's newest search engine and its search algorithms are now being used to power Live, Yahoo!, MSN, and other Microsoft sites. Bing calls itself a "Decision Engine". It is supposed to help make decisions easier by taking into account multiple items such as location and other words you specify in your search. Thus if you type in the words, "pizza Orlando" it gives you only relevant information. What is interesting is that Bing knows if you are referring to Ontario, California, where I happen to be, versus Ontario, Canada based on my IP and other information, as shown in Figure 1.2.

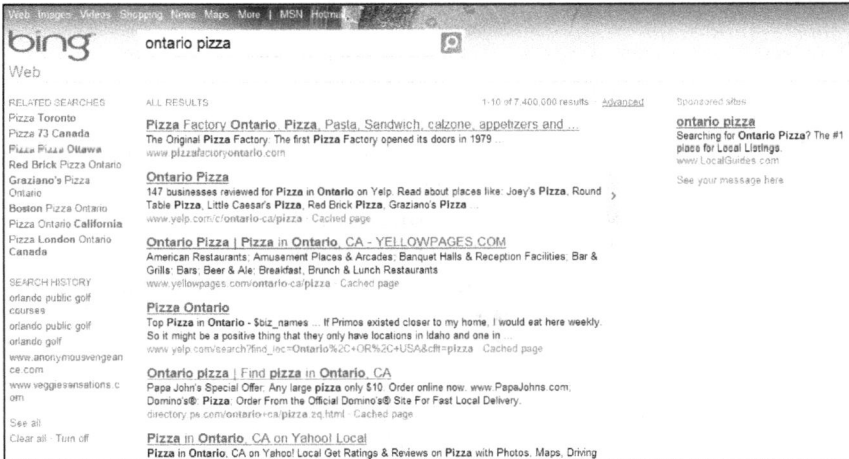

Figure 1.2

Notice that I did not specify any address or whether it was for Ontario, California, or Ontario, Canada. But the results not only gave me Ontario, California pizza places. It is absolutely amazing how far search engines have come and how fast their advanced algorithms work.

> **Good to Know:** When you type in a string of words to get relevant results and then click search, the collection of pages you see with the results are called *search engine results pages (SERPs)*. The higher your business or entity is in the search results, the more traffic you can expect to generate from searches on those key words.
>
> It has been proven that those in the top 20 get the most clicks, as users typically do not go beyond page 2 of a search. The first three web sites listed in a search, given that the description of the company or product is enticing enough, will land the most clicked visits. Your goal is to get your web site in this top three. If your product or service makes a sale on an average of 1 out of every 10 visitors, the more visits you get the more sales you will make.

In trying to get information on the Bing algorithm, Microsoft spokesperson Carolyn Miller stated, "We have made numerous improvements to our algorithm, focusing on spelling, freshness of results, and core ranking. Our algorithm is changing continuously to provide the best results. Although we have a six month release cycle for major updates, our algorithm is refined everyday to improve the relevance of our results and to better address our users' intent."

To learn more about Bing's search engine, you can watch a video at http://www.decisionengine.com.

On July 29, 2009, Wired.com announced what I am sure Google feared. The title of the news article, "Yahoo Gives Up, Turns Search Over To Bing." This new development puts Microsoft closer to being head to head with Google, who once had over 60 percent of the search engine market before Bing entered the race. Also worthy of note is the 100 million dollars that Microsoft is rumored to have spent on advertising Bing.

In mid-2010 Bing and Yahoo! started to really work together to take on Google. And it is working. Bing is taking away searches and revenue from Google faster than anyone thought possible.

Microsoft's Bing search engine has essentially taken over Yahoo! search results and advertising using its Decision Engine.

Crawlers, Spiders, and Robots (Bots)

We've talked a little bit already about the spiders, crawlers, and robots that come visit your site to see what content you have and see what has changed since its last visit. Some search engines visit your site monthly but others (such as news web sites and sites that host blogs) visit daily or even hourly. How do I know this? Well turn on your TV. The next time a major news story breaks on CNN, check the search engines to see if they have a link to the story. While I was writing this, I had CNN on my television and there was breaking news. It had just been announced 5 minutes before but Google already had links to 3 web sites with the story. Incredibly fast!

Google makes it easy to see when its Googlebot has last visited a webpage. You need the Google Toolbar to view this, however. The Google toolbar is available free of charge at http://toolbar.google.com. You download a small program, and you are ready for some easy searching. The toolbar works with Microsoft Windows NT, 2000, XP, Vista, 2003 Server, 2008 Server and Windows 7. You must also need to have Microsoft Internet Explorer version 5.0 or greater installed. There is also a similar version available for Firefox users. Unfortunately, Mac users are still out of luck.

If you have the Google toolbar installed there is a plethora of additional tools and options you can configure including a tool called "PageRank." When you hit the check mark to place the PageRank box on the toolbar as shown in Figure 1.3 you see a small but very powerful rectangular box that is added on the Google Toolbar right next to the Bookmarks button.

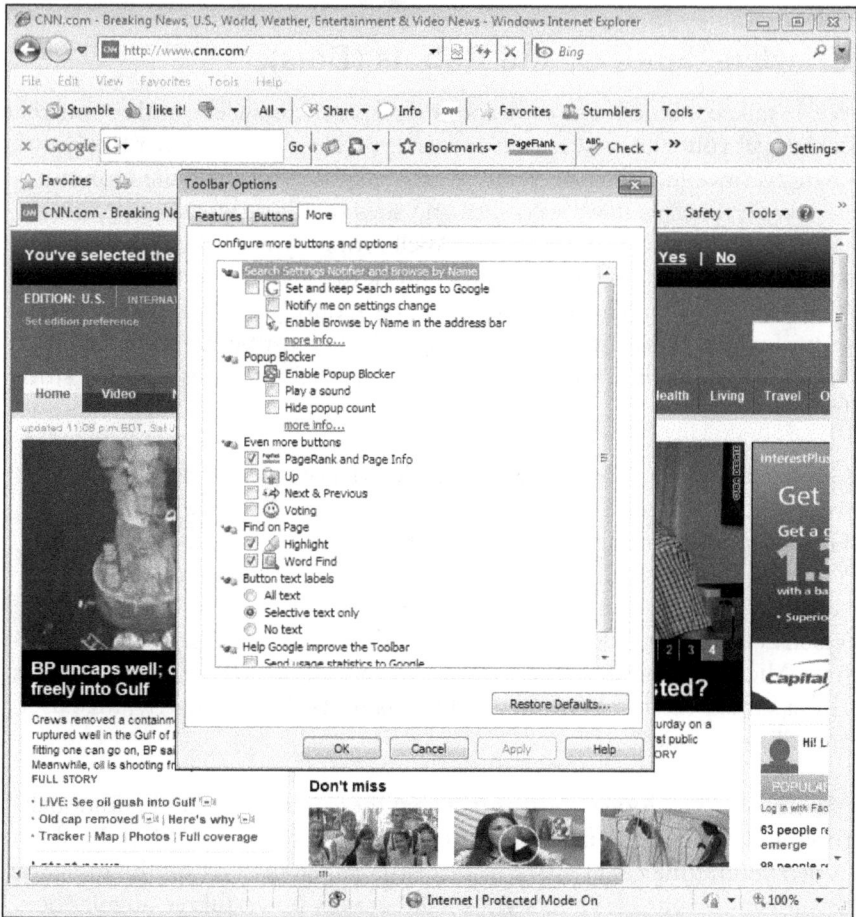

Figure 1.3

The PageRank is in essence the term *quality scoring*. Google's PageRank is a score of a web site from zero to ten (0-10). Ten is the highest and zero is the lowest. If you are competing against another web site on the same keywords, the web site with the higher PageRank will be higher on the SERP page when a search is performed. When you are higher on a page due to your Google page ranking, you have obtained this search. Organic listings are listings you never pay money to the search engines, but your web site was at the top of the search engine results.

Google makes a ranking of a web site based on the factors we have already discussed and some we will discuss later in this book. After the crawlers, spiders, and robots have gathered data from all the sites known on the web, it uses this information to determine a sites page ranking.

This ranking or scoring determination is one of the most secretive parts of SEO.

The goal is to score pages based on the quality and relevance that site visitors derive from each page they visit. How good it looks visually has virtually no effect on what the crawler, spiders, and robots gather from a web site, as shown on the Google PageRank tool below.

> **Note:** *There once was a time when the keywords in the Meta tag made up the rank of a page and was the most important factor. Now they make up about one percent of the Google page ranking. Keywords are still important in web page rankings. However, they're just one of a hundred or so elements that are taken into consideration.*

I know the major influences of this score from experience and from information provided by Google and other search engines. Google as well as the other major search engines are masters of changing their algorithms and the elements that weigh in to their algorithm used to determine the PageRank of each URL. It changes so often that there will probably be a SEO Secrets Book 2012, 2013, and so on.

Google looks at more than the sheer volume of visits a page receives or the number of links to that page from other web sites. It also looks at the pages that direct traffic or have links to your site. If you looked at it from a point system, certain types of web sites (such as news sites, government sites, education sites, and sites Google has already ranked highly) give your web site more points. Accumulate enough points and Google starts to rank your page. Accumulate more and Google increases your page ranking.

A web page that has multiple links to it might rank lower than a page that has just a single link from a "more important" page. It is always good to create pages visitors like, but be mindful of search engines.
Want to know how your page ranks? Let's take a look at how we can view this information and much more using the PageRank Tool from the Google Tool Bar.

Google Toolbar PageRank Tool

Now let's get to the Google PageRank tool and see how useful this tool really is. It has 4 main features. Let's take a look at each one.

1.   The first really cool feature is the rectangular box. It is like a gauge every time you visit a new web site and if you hover over the PageRank box with your mouse, it shows you the site's Google PageRank, as shown on my web site www.WebSEOPros.com (Figure 1.4).

Figure 1.4

Notice in Figure 1.4 that my web site has a page ranking of 7/10. It takes a long time and a lot of work to do everything necessary to gain a 7/10 ranking. Even more to keep the ranking.

Without professional SEO help I find most web sites which have a decent web developer and have been up a long time get a maximum Google ranking of 2 or 3. This is usually far below your competition.

The second feature actually has two parts to it. This is where you can tell on any web site that Google has come to visit the site. If you click the little down arrow next the PageRank box you will see the first of three options—"Caches Snapshot of The Page." Every time the Googlebot visits, it takes a picture of the page as shown in Figure 1.5.

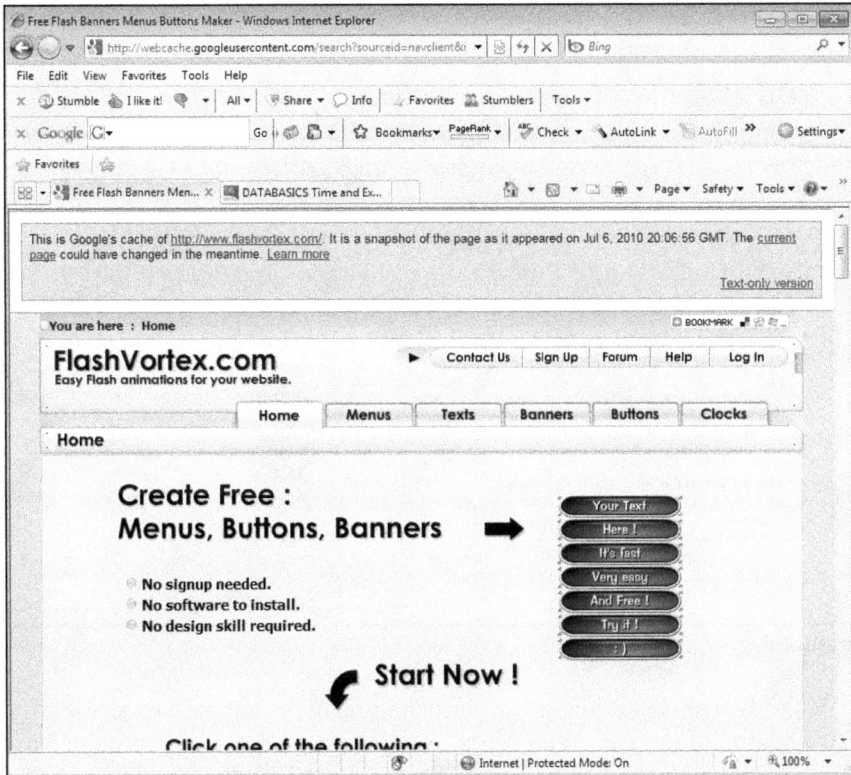

Figure 1.5

Along with a picture of the web site, the time and date of the snapshot is also logged. You also have one other important tool here! Notice to the right a little link that say "Text-only version." Click this and see what the spiders, crawlers, and bots really see (Figure 1.6).

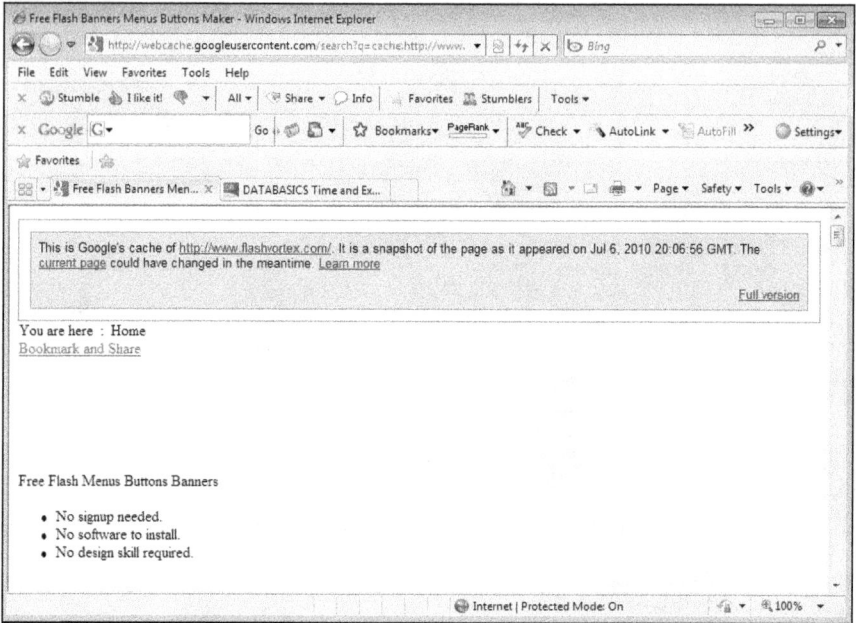

Figure 1.6

It is amazing to see how little text relating to their web site is found on some web pages. All the text on the site is contained in the pictures. I have one customer who had the most awesome-looking web site. It was all done in flash.

However, she had a page ranking of zero, even though she had had the web site up for 8 years. Her web site was better-looking and more interactive than all of her competition.

Nonetheless, her competition was at the top of the organic searches and winning all the clicks, whereas she was at the bottom.

When she became a customer, you can't even imagine how upset she was when I told her we would have to limit the flash and include text instead to get her rankings up. It is hard for some people to understand why flashy isn't always better.

The third feature is called, "Similar Pages" (Figure 1.7).

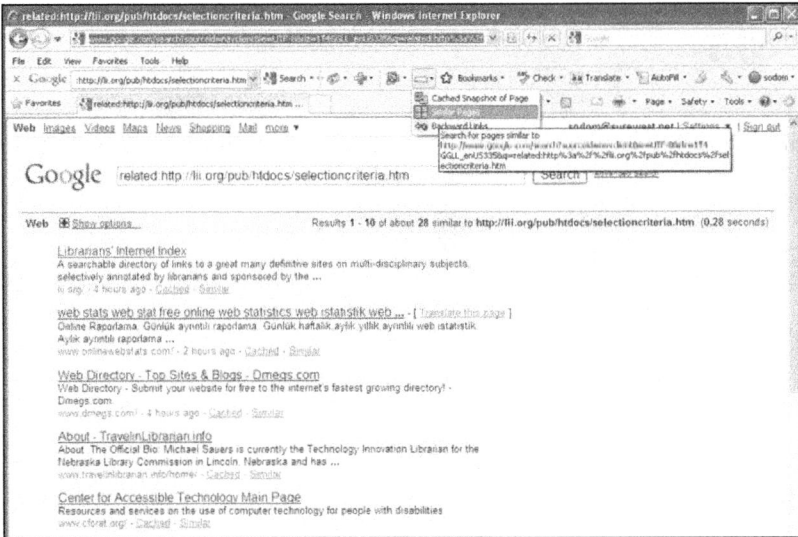

Figure 1.7

The Similar Pages option provides you with, not surprisingly, links to pages which Google deems similar; these links are prime candidates for link exchanges which we will talk about later in this book. Since Google already believes they are related to your industry. The more relevant the links to and from your web site are, the higher Google will make your PageRank score.

2. The last feature you will find on the Google PageRank Tool is the "Backwards Link" option (Figure 1.8).

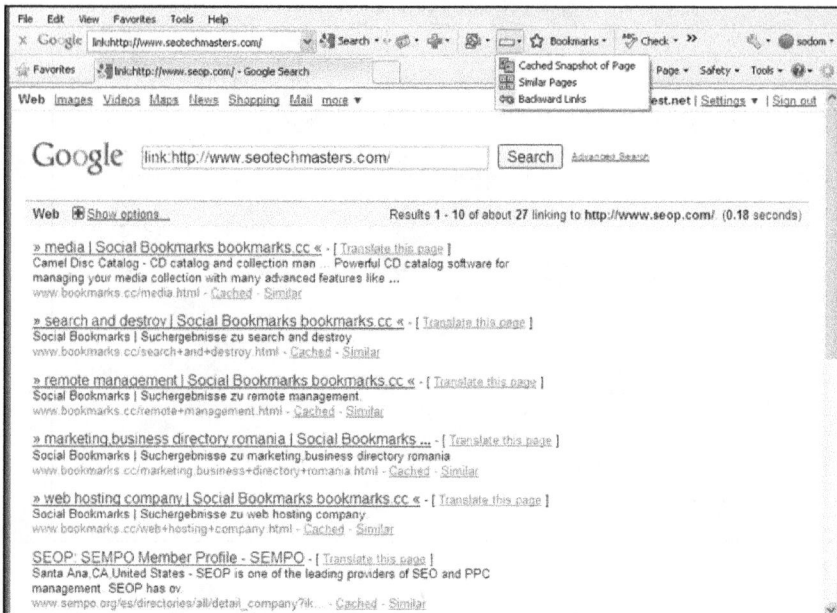

Figure 1.8

> The Backwards Links option takes you to a list of links that the Googlebot has found that link directly to your web site. These are very important to know. The more of these from relevant sites that Google knows about, the higher your PageRank will be.

There is a lot to cover in this book, so let's get started in the next chapter with understanding Meta Tags

Chapter 2 - Keywords and Meta Tags

Keyword Meta tags are no longer a requirement for major search engines as they now scan the actual relevant content that is on every page of your web site. (We already touched on this, but very flashy web sites might find themselves on page 200 of a keyword search simply because crawlers cannot read them, even if their content is relevant.)

Now I said keywords are not a requirement, but I wouldn't leave them out. If you are looking at this from a point perspective, your description, keywords, and other information in your Meta tags all give you more points if they match the content on the landing pages of your web site and the title bar. It all adds up to what the search engines see as relevant content.

In this chapter, we will look at how to properly format Meta tags to allow prime optimization, allow the bots, spiders, and crawlers to visit more than your landing page, how to make them relevant to your keywords, add location-based meta data, and much more!

Keywords

As I said earlier, keywords in your Meta tags are just one of about three dozen elements that are taken into consideration when search engines visit your web site to collect information about your web site. But choosing those keywords and correctly placing those keywords on your web sites landing pages and matching them to the Title and the Meta tagging of your web site absolutely is important.

Some keywords absolutely have value; more importantly, if not used properly, keywords can cause damage to your web site's reputation and make it almost invisible.

Choosing Quality Keywords, or "Trophy Words"

Targeting your trophy keywords is absolutely important!

It's complicated I know. As I said earlier, keywords in Meta tags are no longer a requirement. When I say it is not a requirement, I see companies with a ranking of one or two on Google all the time that don't have a single Meta tag. They don't have a description either.

Their domain's longevity, linkage, and relevant content sped them along in the process to get ranked. But it won't get them much farther in the ranking process. Each stepping stone that you make on the list gets you a little higher in the ranking process.

I always like to explain to customers that each item you do equals a point value to the major search engines.

➢ Have a web site that has been online for a long period, add points.
➢ Have your web site registration paid so it expires in 5 years, add points.
➢ Have it expire in less than a year, subtract points.
➢ Have Meta Tags, add points.
➢ Have relevant content, add points, have quality and relevant links, add points.
➢ Have an SEO company that is a Google Ambassador, add points.
➢ Have news articles published about your web site, add points.
➢ Have links from .gov and .edu sites, add points.
➢ Have a good web site quality score, add points.
➢ Do well on all 150 factors I outline here in this book, get higher rankings!

The higher the point values, the higher the rankings can become. Points are based on a number of factors: the industry you're in, the competition you have, competing companies with SEO vying for the top spots, local or national campaigns, traffic to your web site, two way links, and much more, but obviously not based on your keywords alone. In fact, keywords barely have an impact on rankings.

(However, keywords have a major impact on quality scoring, which you will learn a lot about in this book.)

Even though, the keywords you decide to use in the Meta tags only make a small difference in relevancy and rankings on search engines, if you use those keywords in different places in your web site to make your word density higher, they have a more noticeable impact and your web site will seem more relevant to the search engines. In fact here is a chart we have put together to show just how much of an impact on relevancy placing your keywords on your web site can be:

1. Keyword in the Title Tag   (6%)
2. Keyword as the first word(s) of the Title Tag   (6%)
3. Keyword in the Root Domain Name (e.g. keyword.com)   (6%)
4. Keyword in the H1 Headline Tag   (5%)
5. Keyword in Internal Link Anchor Text on the Page   (4%)
6. Keyword in External Link Anchor Text on the Page   (4%)
7. Keyword in the H1 Tag   (4%)
8. Keyword in the First 100 Words in HTML on the Page   (4%)
9. Keyword in a sub domain (bestwines.vinolist.com) (4%)

10. Keyword in the page name URL
    (ww.vinolist.com/bestwines.html)   (3%)
11. Keyword in other H Tags (3%)
12. Keyword in image ALT text   (3%)
13. Keyword repeating in the HTML Text on the Page   (3%)
14. Keyword in image names on the page (keyword.jpg)   (3%)
15. Keyword in <b> or <strong> tags   (2%)
16. Keyword in List Items <li> on the Page   (3%)
17. Keyword in <i> or <em> Tags   (2%)
18. Keyword in the Meta Description Tag   (2%)
19. Keyword in comment tags in the HTML   (1%)
20. Keyword in the Meta tagging (5%)

This information is average relational information which we have
gathered here at Web SEO Pros by targeting Google's results from our
experimental optimization. This information often changes slightly from
month to month and industry to industry. Algorithms and requirements
change so much nowadays that we are now publishing this book every
year with the new updates. It's worth it to keep up with the changes every
year. Particularly this year because of the introduction of the Bing search
engine.

Long-Tail Keywords

Long-tail keywords are a type of keyword phrase that have at least two,
and some times as many as five, words in the phrase. Long-tail keywords
are used to refine search terms to the web page, as well as to cater to
those who are looking for something rather specific. Like normal
keywords, long-tail keywords are used to define what is on the web page
and what the publisher wants to be found under in search engines and on
search engine results pages.

These keywords are highly specific and draw less traffic for the web site.
However, they tend to draw more quality traffic, which leads to more
conversions (sales) than normal keywords. Long-tail keywords can also be
used by the web site creator and visitors in different ways.

When the web site creator uses long-tail keywords, they are searching to
corner a market that might be smaller than normal, but has just as much
potential as other larger, more exposed markets. Using long-tail keywords
can also be less expensive when it comes to pay-per-click bidding and
other paid inclusion methods, as there are less people attempting to place
bids on those keywords for pay per click ads on search engine results
pages.

Visitors use long-tail keywords to narrow down what they are searching for. For example, let's say you sell pizza's in the Orlando Florida area. Potential clients will most likely search for you under the long-tail keywords, "orlando pizza restaurants" It makes sense for you as a web site owner to use those same long-tail keywords in your optimization.

To successfully use long-tail keywords, a web site creator needs to know which long-tail keywords actually get hits or are searched for on the major search engines. Research is the only way to know if long-tail keywords will work or not, and if the smaller investment in longer keywords will still pay off at the end of the marketing campaign.

Keyword Stuffing

I can see what you are thinking right now. As a web site owner you're probably jotting down a list of every word you can think of as a keyword for someone to search with to find your web site. I had a private eye who came to me for SEO services and he had more keywords in his Meta tagging than on his whole web site. When we were done deciding on the eight he would use, we didn't even use one of the keywords he had on his list before he came to me.

His list, I kid you not, had every city in Southern California with every possible scenario for which you might need a private investigator. He had probably close to a thousand keywords—this is an extreme example of what is known as "keyword stuffing."

As a consultant I spend countless hours finding and applying the right keywords for my customers and working with those who design web sites for my customers. Finding the most effective keywords is a fine science and I have to weigh using popular and effective keywords on a web site against the amount of competition. When I get done with a web site, I have eight to twelve keywords I focus on; I call these words, "Trophy Words." I use these words to improve your site's ranking.

Let me give an example. I do the SEO for a web site that gives multiple types of counseling to patients. The keyword, "reno family counseling," is a term that is searched on about 2,500 times per month in Reno, Nevada. However, there are 2,000 counselors with web sites that are competing for the same keyword in the region.

On the other hand, there are 1,250 searches in Reno for "reno divorce counseling," but only about 100 therapists with web sites competing for that term. This is a small example, but you can see I would choose the second keyword term over the first even though there are fewer searches, but only after taking into consideration the site rankings of the competition (discussed later in this chapter).

Determining Your Trophy Keywords

We have talked about the keywords and what they can do for you, but picking the right keywords is, well, the key.

If you are a small-business owner, you will want your web site to be readily visible on each and every search engine for the right keywords. In fact using the right keywords in your web site's content can mean the difference between being listed as one of the first 20 sites returned from search engine results (which is good) or being buried under other web sites forty pages into the results, which means hundreds of results are returned before someone sees your site.

There have been many studies showing that searchers rarely venture past the second page of searches on a search engine and the majority choose web sites on the first page of the results when looking for something online.

So how many keywords do I choose? Well you want to choose as many as you need to draw people to your web site. As long as they are relevant to your web site and avoid "Head Keywords".

Head Keywords are short one or two word concepts that can have a wide range of meanings. They have a high volume of searches, but the variety of possible meanings makes it difficult to know what the user was actually searching for. An example of head keyword would be the word **golf**. What are you marketing? Tee times? Golf shoes? Golf clubs? You get the point.

After you pick your keywords you want to target a maximum of 1 to trophy keywords for each landing page. If you have any more the major search engines will penalize you and you may be creating keywords that are too broad.

This is actually a major change and one of the reasons I rewrite this book every single year. My book in 2009 said you could focus on 10-12 keywords, my book in 2010 said you could focus on 8-12. During the middle of 2010 web site pages focusing on more than 3 keywords started dropping in the rankings and we had to do some major redesigns of a lot of our customers web sites to maintain their rankings and positions on keywords. Part of this can be contributed to Google Caffeine which we will also discuss later in this book.

> **NOTE:** *When you are done with this chapter, you will learn that in order to be the most effective on search engines you can only focus on 1 to 3 keywords per landing page. So what do you do when you have many more keywords? The answer can be found in Chapter 14.*

Another significant change is the addition of negative keywords in high competition industries. For instance. I focus on a web site for the keyword "Disneyland Golf". Disneyland is actually in Santa Ana California and my clients golf course is near Huntington Beach about 15 minutes away.

I had the golfing web site number one for Google and Bing for a long time. Suddenly they lost relevancy and started dropping. Luckily I have a system that checks every keyword and it's standings weekly and noticed the web site drop 7 positions on Google in one week. I have never seen this before from any of my clients so highly ranked.

Usually a sudden drop in the rankings indicates another company is now competing against me with SEO or a news story about a competitor dropped us down. None of this was the case after reviewing the competition. In a few weeks I figured out that Google had implemented a negative keyword change in their algorithm.

After we did an algorithm review of the web site we figured out that the word "Huntington Beach" on the web site now added negative points to the search. So many negative points that all the optimization in the world wouldn't bring them to the top of search engines for the keyword of "Disneyland Golf".

So how did I fix it? It is way out of the scope of this chapter and because of so many new changes I had to add a new chapter in the book. The solution to this problem and many others relating to higher numbers of keywords are found later in this book.

We need to get back on track now. I am going to do a few more examples of "Head Keywords". Let's say you have a web site that reviews films and rates them. If your only keyword is "films," that is too broad. Do you sell films? Do you develop them? Do you make them? Do you have cleaning products to clean different films? No. You have to make your keywords more relevant. Now if one of my keywords in my Meta tagging was "feature film critic" or "feature film reviews," then that would be more relevant. Notice that a keyword is more like a key phrase than a word.

There are two ways of keyword stuffing. One is by being too broad on your Meta keywords and having way more than three keywords or so. Let's say that you own a convenience store and you put a list of products you carry (such as donuts, sodas, fountain drinks, bottled drinks, ice drinks, etc.) as keywords. You would be stuffing your keywords.

The other way of keyword stuffing is using the keywords you have too many times in your content. This is an extreme example of keyword spamming, but let's say you have the convenience store and to make your web site seem really relevant, you take the list of your keywords and you put them on your web sites landing page 500 times at the end of your page.

Let's say you make the wording the same color as your web site's background so that you are hiding it from the human visitors using your web site. Well not only are the bots, crawlers, and spiders smart enough to find it and penalize you for it, you might wind up on the list of web sites that got banned from Google for doing things just like that.

Being banned from Google is like being blacklisted from the Internet. You are better off getting a new domain, domain hosting, and company name and starting over.

I like to give my customers this example. When you are typing in Microsoft Word, and the red underline points out misspellings and the green underline points out incomplete sentences, the spiders, bots, and crawlers can see the same thing. They know when your content doesn't makes sense, contains errors, and is not relevant to human eyes. They will penalize you for doing it and you may not even know it.

Understanding How Keywords Are Used

It helps to decide on keywords if you understand how people search the Internet using search engines. When you go to a search engine and want a hair perm, you open a search engine such as Google and you type in "hair salon" and hit search. You get about 268,000 results but none of them are places you can go locally and get a perm.

Are you going to go searching through the 268,000 results for a local place to get a hair service? Not likely. You're going to refine your search down to something less broad like like the city which you are looking for the hair salon like, "orlando hair salon" which will have better results.

If I have the salon in Orlando and I want to optimize my website I would make one of my keywords "Orlando hair salon". I would have less of a chance of getting the visitors I wanted to my web site if I separated the words and made the Meta tags "orlando, hair, salon" as these are more broad and have less relevance to the search if they are treated as individual keywords. Each word separated by a comma is treated by most search engines as an individual search term because of the comma is a Meta tag delimiter.

Orlando is a city, hair could refer to any number of hair items or services, brushes, hair bands, combs, etc. We can keep going on but I think I have made the point here. Using the exact phrase people will use as a search term in your keywords can make all the difference on whether your site will show up on a search engine search.

A few more tips:

- **Singular vs. plural keywords**—Search engines and keyword research tools handle singular and plural terms differently. **Cherry** will return different search results than **Cherries.**

- **Word order and prominence is critical**—The order of the words that are typed into a search box does matter. The search term **"tea cup"** has different results than **"tea cups".**

Keyword Research Tools

There are many tools on the Internet to help you find the exact keywords to use for your web site. The trick is understanding how keywords work, which you should use, and the best ways to use them. If you choose the most relevant keywords and properly design your site using those keywords you will have a highly visible and successful web site.

At a basic level, keywords capture the essence of your web site. Keywords are the words or phrases a potential visitor to your site enters into a search engine to find web site related to the specific subject matter they are looking for. If you went to Google and did a search and had to go through 30 pages of content to find a web site the matched what you were looking for, you would stop using Google and go back to the telephone book, or choose Yahoo! instead. That is why choosing keywords that match your web site's content are so important. The keywords that you choose are used throughout the optimization process applied to your web site. And if they aren't, well then don't expect to have anyone find your web site, unless they know the exact URL to find it.

- So let's ask ourselves some questions:
- What words best describe my web site content?
- How do I know which keywords to use?
- Where do I find help in deciding?
- Once I know my possible keywords, where do I see how many people search on those keywords?

All of these are great questions and knowing the answers to these questions will save you a great deal of time when creating a web site.

First off you can go to Google and start to type words that apply to your site. The most commonly searched terms will populate for you as shown in Figure 2.1, where I began to search for "sacramento pizza".

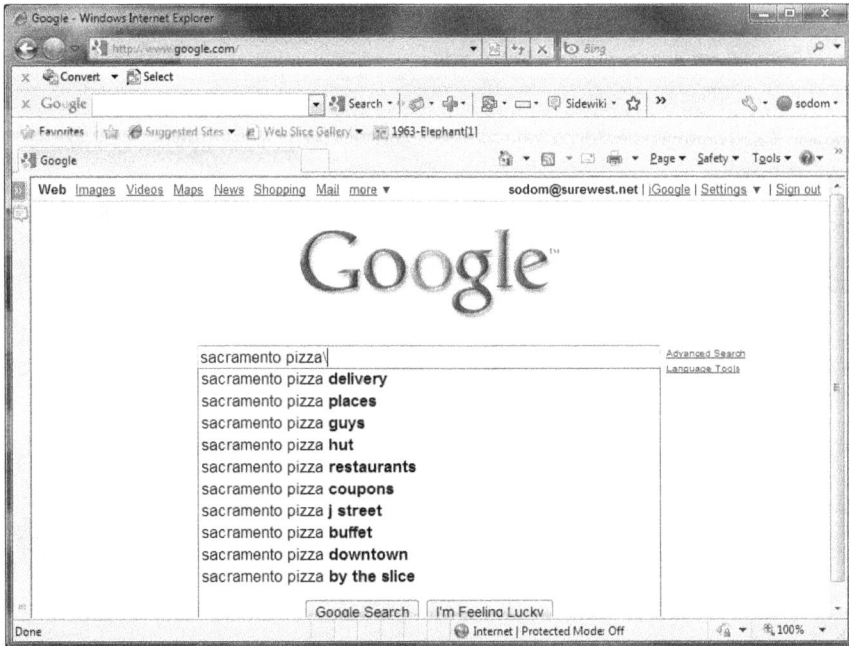

Figure 2.1

There are five hundred software packages, books, and web sites out there to help you determine your keywords. One of the best, if you want all the work done for you, is www.SubmissionComplete.com.

However, if you don't want to spend the money, do what I do. Have Google do the work for you. "Say what? Google do the work for me?" you ask.

Google has a little known web site tool for determining keywords. They advertised its existence to Google Ambassadors and Adwords custoemrs but it is generally unknown to most web site owners and the general public. Let's take a look at what this tool can do for you.

Why is it the best? Well only Google can tell you how many searches were performed in a given month for a specific keyword and how much competition there is for each search. This tool gives you all of that information!

If you go to the URL of:

https://adwords.google.com/select/KeywordToolExternal

You will find this tool as shown in Figure 2.2.

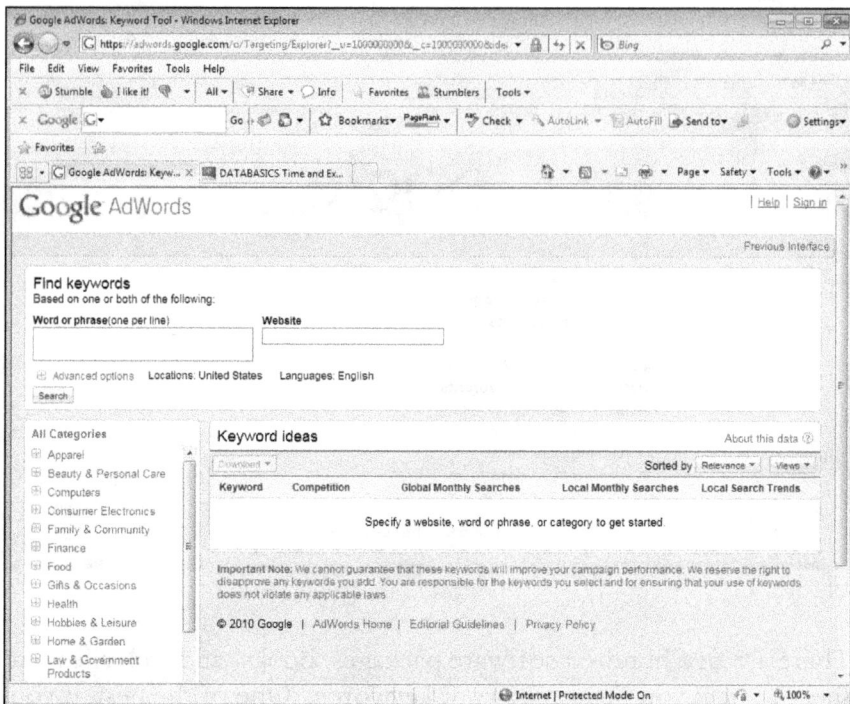

Figure 2.2

Notice you have a couple of options. You can enter a generalization of your keywords or, if you already have a web site, you can choose to have Google crawl your web site and decide the words that might work for you.

The search reply that you get back will be incredibly long and many of the results will most likely not apply to your web site. Of the ones that do apply, you will be able to see an average of the number of searches done on a local or global level. Not only that, but you can see a measurement of how stiff the competition is for each keyword!

Let's take a look at both options in detail.

Google General Keyword Search Tool

Now it's not called the Google General Keyword Search Tool, but I had to have a descriptive name in the title. I am fortunate enough to have a very large alternative news site as a client, and so I will use the search term "alternative news" as shown in Figure 2.3.

Figure 2.3

Here are the results in Figures 2.4 and 2.5.

Find keywords
Based on one or both of the following:

Word or phrase(one per line)   Website

palm beach plumbing

⊞ Advanced options   Locations: United States   Languages: English

Search

All Categories	**Keyword ideas** Sign in with your AdWords login information to see the full set of ideas for this search.

⊞ Apparel
⊞ Beauty & Personal Care
⊞ Computers
⊞ Consumer Electronics
⊞ Family & Community
⊞ Finance
⊞ Food
⊞ Gifts & Occasions
⊞ Health
⊞ Hobbies & Leisure
⊞ Home & Garden
⊞ Law & Government Products
⊞ Media & Events

Contains
Sort: **Alphabetical** | Highest count

☑ All

About this data ⑦

Download ▾   Sorted by Relevance ▾   Views ▾

Keyword			Competition	Global Monthly Searches	Local Monthly Searches	Local Search Trends
palm beach plumbing	◎			2,400	2,400	
palm beach plumbers	◎			1,300	1,000	
things to do palm beach	◎			6,600	6,600	
next plumbing	◎			1,000	-	-
plumbing help	◎			6,600	4,400	
hughes plumbing	◎			2,400	1,900	
palm beach wedding	◎			18,100	14,800	
palm beach plumbing parts	◎			170	-	-
palm beach attractions	◎			27,100	27,100	

Figure 2.4

Additional keywords to consider - sorted by relevance ⑦				
weekly		5,000,000	5,000,000	Add
alternative press		40,500	40,500	Add
alternative tv		5,400	14,800	Add
alternative media		12,100	33,100	Add
news local		1,220,000	1,220,000	Add
independent news		22,200	60,500	Add
alternative journalism		390	720	Add
abc news		1,500,000	1,830,000	Add
newspaper		11,100,000	16,600,000	Add
newspapers		2,740,000	5,000,000	Add
alternative weekly		Not enough data	4,400	Add
news tv stations		12,100	12,100	Add
news station		90,500	90,500	Add
tv news		550,000	823,000	Add
weather news		165,000	246,000	Add
nbc news		550,000	550,000	Add
news abc		1,500,000	1,830,000	Add
headlines news		110,000	201,000	Add
television news		60,500	74,000	Add
ads news		22,200	22,200	Add
music news		135,000	246,000	Add
publications news		6,600	8,100	Add
alternative television		Not enough data	720	Add
natural news		22,200	22,200	Add
community news		60,500	60,500	Add
health news		246,000	201,000	Add
news headlines		110,000	201,000	Add
alternative station		5,400	6,600	Add
advertising news		22,200	22,200	Add
news channel		2,740,000	2,740,000	Add
magazine news		110,000	135,000	Add
news daily		2,740,000	2,740,000	Add
circulation news		8,100	8,100	Add
papers news		165,000	550,000	Add
usnpl news		Not enough data	58	Add
news weekly		60,500	110,000	Add

Figure 2.5

Notice in Figure 2.5 that the keyword tool also provides related suggestive keywords. These are possible keywords you may not have thought about. Also the list can be downloaded in either a text, .csv (for MS Excel), or .csv formats to review later.

Now let's look at what happens if I let Google crawl the site and come up with search terms.

Google Crawler Keyword Search Tool

Again, the title of this section is not an official name for their search tool. I am going to use one of my customer's web sites called *localnewsday.com*. I haven't asked their permission to be in the book, but I do a good enough job that I don't think they will care, and since they are reeling over the fact that they had over 16,000 unique hits last month, my competition will have a hard time wooing them as a client.

So let's use them. In Figure 2.6, I chose to have Google crawl the site to determine the best keywords to use.

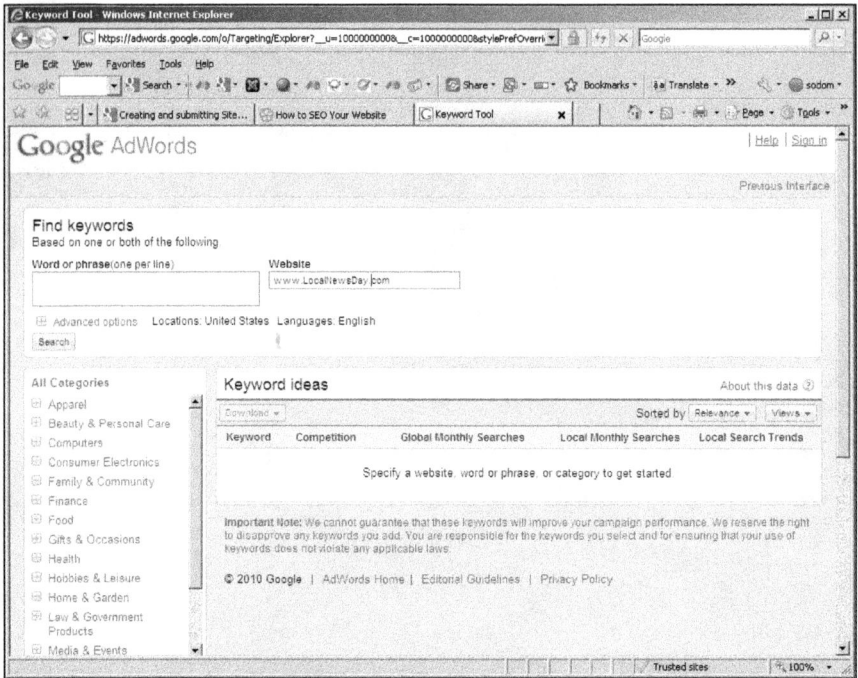

Figure 2.6

When it gets done let's take a look at Figure 2.7 to see what the differences are. If you have ever used this tool before, you will notice that the look has completely changed and Google has just added a Local Search Trend which shows a graph of how much more or less searches take place in a given month for the particular keyword.

Figure 2.7

Sometimes you will notice that some of the keywords don't fit, like the keyword of "health insurance" which showed up when I did a keyword search of Local News Day. At first this caught me off guard until I went to the web site and saw that there was a news story related to health insurance as shown in Figure 2.8.

Figure 2.8

The news stories and links currently on the web site will also explain some of the miscellaneous keywords that Google came up with in Figure 2.9.

Keyword	Competition		Global Monthly Searches	Local Monthly Searches	Local Search Trends
local news			1,500,000	1,000,000	
portland local news			3,600	3,600	
portland tv stations			2,900	2,900	
portland news channel			12,100	-	-
news headlines			368,000	110,000	
portland or news			6,600	6,600	
news channels			135,000	60,500	
portland or local news			480	-	-
tv stations			450,000	368,000	
star news			550,000	201,000	
portland breaking news			1,600	1,600	
portland news stations			1,300	-	-
portland newspapers			6,600	6,600	
latest news			4,090,000	1,220,000	
daily news			3,350,000	2,740,000	
portland or breaking news		-	170	-	-
newspaper headlines			90,500	40,500	
news stations			165,000	165,000	
tv news			1,500,000	550,000	
northwest cable news			2,900	2,400	
portland tv news			880	-	-
portland daily news			170	-	-
portland or news stations		-	210	-	-
portland news			74,000	74,000	
republic newspaper			40,500	40,500	
news paper			3,350,000	823,000	
breaking news			1,500,000	823,000	

Figure 2.9

How to Decide the Trophy Words

Well, you have collected the information you need to decide on your trophy keywords for your web site but probably not which ones to use. You know the possible keywords, the number of local and global searches, and an estimate of how much competition there is for those keywords.

As I said before, as a consultant I spend countless hours finding and applying the right keywords for my customers and working with those who design web sites for my customers. Finding the most effective keywords is a fine science and sometimes it's an experimental process.

Many times I will add, subtract and reorder my Meta tagged keywords based on what is working and what is not on my customers web sites. I can tell a lot about how well a keyword is working by tracking a Pay-Per-Click (PPC) campaign. But we will discuss that later in this book.

Now that I have my possible keyword list from Google in the last section, I have to weigh using heavily searched keywords against the amount of competition I have. If I have a high Google ranking I can compete against whoever I want for the keywords, but if I am just starting out and my ranking is low on Google, I have to choose words that have less competition.

If I went right out for the search term "daily news" as shown in Figure 2.7 for my customer LocalNewsDay.com it would be a big mistake. Sure, there are 2.7 million searches a month for that term but there are 600 sites ranked higher than LocalNewsDay.com's site and it would wind up on page 43 of any Google search for that term.

On the other hand, if I went for the search term "Orlando daily news," there is a good chance that even with a low ranking I will wind up on page 1 or 2 with basic optimization in a few months because there is less competition for that search term.

Meta Description

The description is what most people see on the end of a Google search. Right under the link to the web site page is the Meta tagging description. Now that you have decided on your keywords, you now need to formulate your keywords into your description using complete sentences. This is not as easy as it sounds.

If you use long-tail keywords you must use them in the same order in your description. Additionally, you need to keep your descriptions to 155 characters or less. This is the number of characters most search engines will display.

Let's give some examples:

Orlando excavating, Orlando excavation, Orlando dump truck, Orlando tight access excavating, Orlando residential landscaping, Orlando trackhoe,loader.

Now the description should be:

We are Orlando excavating professionals who can handle any Orlando excavation jobs needing a dump truck, tight access track hoe or loader. Whether you are doing landscaping or clearing a site we come with a full size dump truck, track hoe, and loader all at one great price.

Meta Title tags

Your title may be one of the most important parts of your web site, as shown at the top of Figure 2.10.

Figure 2.10

Remember those keywords you decided on? You want to use as many of those (and in the same order) as you can. Google allows up to 66 characters (including spaces) for title tags, whereas some others look at up to 120 characters. The numbers change frequently; last year the general rule was no more than 70 characters.

If your title tags exceed those limits, they'll be truncated to fit into the maximum space allowed. To ensure that you're getting the most value for the character limitations of title tags, the World Wide Web Consortium (W3C) recommends that web site designers keep their titles to 64 characters or less in length.

In Figure 2.11 you see the title tag which appears below. In the next section we will show you how to configure the Title as well as the rest of the Meta tags.

Figure 2.11

You notice again at the top of Figure 2.11 that the title looks a lot like keywords. Why? Because it is! You should use as many of your keywords as you can in your title, and in the order that they are listed in your Meta tags.

Search engine crawlers, bots, and spiders use these title tags as one of the main source for determining the web-page topic. Spiders, bots, and crawlers examine the title and the words used in it, and then uses this information as a key source to determine the topic of the page. It's always best to use your keywords in your page title, and to use them as close to the beginning of the title as possible.

There should also be unique Title tags for every page of your web site. This creates relevancy and distinguishes the difference in content. Make the title as descriptive as possible and use the most important keywords you've decided on for the page. Words you use in your Title tag will appear in the reverse title bar, or the tab title, of your web browser, as well.

Using Meta Tags To Allow Spider, Bots, and Crawlers

Did you know that the search engines don't usually send their creepy crawlers to index your site without your permission? This is one of the biggest mistakes web site owners make.

I can see many of you reading this have your eyes wide open, asking yourself if you have done this part! It is a good question to ask because I would say 7 out of 10 people desperate for my SEO help don't have this done and anything else they do doesn't make a difference.

There are two ways you can allow spiders, bots, and crawlers to come index your site. You can include a file called robot.txt with permissions (discussed later in the book) or you can use the Meta Robots tags, which is the most efficient way. If you haven't done this, you might see your landing page on a web site, but you will never see a good ranking and none of your other pages will get indexed.

> **Sidebar: The Meta Robots Tag**
> The gives you the ability to specify whether search engine bots, spiders, and crawlers can index that page or follow the links appearing on that page.
> The following is the Meta Robots tag which should be on your landing page. (You will learn where to put your Meta tags in the next section.) I add it to every page of the web site:
> `<meta name="robots" content="index,follow">`
> There are other syntaxes you can use instead of "index.follow." They are as follows:
> > **index:** This allows the spider to index that page.
> > **noindex:** This instructs the spider not to index the page.
> > **follow:** This instructs the spider to follow the links from that page and index them.
> > **nofollow:** This instructs the spider not to follow links from that page for indexing.
> >
> > **all:** This is identical to "index, follow".
> >
> > **none:** This is identical to "noindex, nofollow" telling the search engines to ignore the web page.

The other acceptable tags:

```
<meta name="robots" content="noindex,follow">
<meta name="robots" content="index,nofollow">
<meta name="robots" content="noindex,nofollow">
<meta name="robots" content="all">
<meta name="robots" content="none">
```

Keep in mind that you can only use one of the tags. They are not used in combination with each other.

Configuring Meta Tags

You already learned earlier in the chapter that your Meta tagging (also known as "long-tail keywords" because they are not usually a single word) starts with determining your keywords. I could go section by section here but let's go and analyze the keywords all at once. I think you might understand it better if I just show you what the keywords should look like and then break it down tag by tag.

So let's say we have an imaginary furniture store called "Orlando Office Stuff." (I did Google that to make sure it wasn't really a business.) At our imaginary business, we sell office and healthcare furniture and do office interiors, cubicles, and furniture installation and repair.

I already did the research and my long-tail keywords are:

- Orlando office furniture
- Orlando office interiors
- Orlando office cubicles

I had a few more I want to use:
- Orlando furniture installers
- Orlando furniture repair
- Orlando healthcare furniture
- Orlando medical furniture
- Teknion
- Steelcase
- Herman Miller

Earlier I told you that the new rule is using 1-3 long-tail keywords on a lading page to keep the page relevant in high competition industries which is just about every industry now. Last year I would have done fine using 8-10, but not anymore. So let's take a look at what I came up with for the title and Meta tagging for this web site.

<HEAD>
<Title> **Orlando Office Furniture | Orlando Office Interiors | Orlando Office Cubicles**</Title>
<Meta http-equiv="Content-type" content="text/html; charset=ISO-8859-1">
<Meta name="keywords" content="**Orlando office furniture, Orlando office interiors, Orlando office cubicles**"">

```
<Meta name="description" content="Orlando Office Stuff is the
premier source for Orlando office furniture, Orlando office
Interiors, and Orlando office cubicles. We service Orlando,
Gresham, and surrounding areas. We specialize in planning and
outfitting your office environment from top to bottom.">
<Meta name="googlebot" content="index, follow" />
<Meta name="robots" content=" index,follow ">
<Meta name="Revist-After" content="7 days">
<Meta name="city" content="Orlando">
<Meta name="country" content="United States (USA)">
<Meta name="state" content="OR">
<Meta name="zip code" content="97210">
<Meta name="subject" content="Orlando Office Furniture">
<Meta name="author" content="Jason McCormick">
<Meta name="copyright" content="Orlando Office Stuff">
</HEAD>
```

(Notice in my description I used every keyword I chose in the order I chose them.)

<Body>
(This is where the visible portion of your web site is configured.)
</Body>

So let's take a look at each one of these in the sections ahead.

Configuring the Keyword Meta Tag

So I am going a little out of order, but I need it to make sense to you and to reiterate what I have been trying to explain through this entire chapter. That is, keywords are IMPORTANT. You shouldn't even think about the Title tag or the Description tag until you have decided on your keywords! In the last section I showed you the keywords that I had decided on. If you don't know how I determined my keywords, I taught you this a few sections back. So the tag is configured like this:

```
<Meta name="keywords" content="Orlando office furniture,
Orlando office interiors, Orlando office cubicles">
```

I made keywords bold for this example. The keywords aren't bolded in the configuration. You might notice something else. All the keywords are in lower case. Why? Well Google doesn't care but you need to think about all the search engines. Some are case sensitive and most people don't capitalize their word searches. They just type in their keywords to search.

Configuring the Meta Title Tag

The title tag is located somewhere in between the opening <head> tag and before the closing <\HEAD> tag. It doesn't really matter where it is, but most people put the Title above the Meta tags.

Now remember our keywords? Notice that I used the first 3 which are my main "trophy words" in the title.

> <Title>**Orlando Office Furniture | Orlando Office Interiors | Orlando Office Cubicles** </Title>

Configuring the GoogleBot and the Robot Tags

Here is the Meta Robots tag that we discussed a few sections back in a sidebar. You might notice another tag though. Google really likes it when you put its own Meta tag in your web site and tell him what to do. That tag is called "googlebot" and the instructions are similar to the Robots tag as shown:

index: This allows the GoogleBot to index that page.

noindex: This tells the GoogleBot not to index the page.

follow: This allows the GoogleBot to follow the links from the landing page and other pages it finds and index them.

nofollow: This instructs the spider not to follow links from that page for indexing.

Noodp: Prevents the search from using the page's description.

The tags are easy and should be in any web site you have. Also, you never know what users or links Googlebot or other creepy crawlers arrive from and so these should be in the Meta tags of every page in your web site.

> <Meta name="googlebot" content="**index, follow**" />
> <Meta name="robots" content=" **index,follow** ">

Configuring the Meta Revisit Tag

Google and other major search engines typically visit your site once per month on average. But let's say your web site's content changes more frequently, such as with a news web site. How do you tell the search engines spiders, bots, and crawlers to visit more frequently? The "Revisit-After" Meta tag is used just for this purpose.

> <Meta name="Revist-After" content="**7 days**">

Configuring the Meta Location Tags

These tags are really important to Bing.com and other search engines to help identify the geographical locations. In a few sections we will look at a new GPS type of geographic location tool and add the Meta tags as well.

In the example below, you add the city, country, state, and zip code, just as if you were mailing yourself a letter, as shown below:

<Meta name="city" content="**Orlando**">
<Meta name="country" content="**United States (USA)**">
<Meta name="state" content="**OR**">
<Meta name="zip code" content="**97210**">

Configuring the Meta Subject Tag

This tag arguably has very little influence with the major search engines but it does have some with the smaller ones. I typically place the first long-tail keywords (again, which should include the most important subject of our web site) in my Meta Keywords tag here, as shown below.

<Meta name="subject" content="**Orlando Office Furniture**">

Configuring the Author and Copyright Meta Tags

These two tags do very little to enhance your search engine rankings and have more to do with identifying who owns all the hard work you put into your web site. I see parts of my books in other books and on the Internet all the time. Most have the common sense to give me credit, but when they don't, I get upset. I spent blood, sweat, and tears to get this done. (Not to mention the time I didn't get to spend with my family because I was writing and doing other things!)

The "author" tag is the person or company name that created the content in the web site. The "copyright" tag identifies who owns the copyright. I will remind all the readers the Orlando Office Stuff, Inc. is entirely bogus and at the time of this writing didn't really exist.

<Meta name="author" content="**Jason McCormick**">
<Meta name="copyright" content="**Orlando Office Stuff, Inc.**">

Meta Redirect Tag

Have you ever wanted to redirect someone to another site when they got to a page? Say you changed your web sites URL. Well you can with just one line! Let's take a look at this one liner:

<Meta http-equiv="refresh" content="**5**;url=**http://www.Orlandooffice stuff.com/blog.html**">

Now the "5" indicates the number of seconds to wait. If you don't want search engines to ding you as if it is a doorway page (which we will discuss later in this book), then it needs to be set to 5 seconds or longer. The last part is the URL that you want to redirect the page to. In the above example I chose the page to be the blog.html page.

NOTE: *There are many other not so important Meta Tags. You can learn them all at: http://www.metatags.info.*

Now let's take a look the new geographical Meta tag that is really catching on using GPS and longitude and latitude.

Adding yourself to GeoURL

Identifying your businesses location in your Meta tags is jumping up in high tech, and Google and other search engines are catching on. GeoURL has started a new Meta tagging system to identify where your business is located. This helps the search engine identify how close you are to a customer and give proper mileage. If you are a retail establishment such as a store or restaurant, doing this can actually help you show up on GPS device searches as well. Let's go to GeoURL in Figure 2.12.

Figure 2.12

First you need to identify where you are. If your web site is about your business you will need the coordinates for your businesses location.

You can go to *http://geourl.org/add/helper* to not only get your coordinates for your tag, but to generate your tags as well if you are in the US, as shown in Figure 2.13.

GeoURL 2.0 – beta

Home | Add your site | Weblog

GeoURL Header Generator

Input your address (only works in the US) and the title for your site and we'll create tags for you to add to your page.

Address examples:
Hollywood & Highland, Los Angeles, CA
155 W 51st St, 10019

Address:
Site title: [Submit]

Go back to the add your site instructions.

Comments to Ask Bjørn Hansen at ask@develooper.com – About this site
This page was generated in 0.00 seconds | Licensed under a Creative Commons License.

Figure 2.13

Remember my fictitious company in the last section. I have made up an address and entered it in to the GeoURL Head Generator and it actually gave me the tags that I need to use with the GPS coordinates for my business.

GPS coordinates are in the form of latitude and longitude, separated by a comma. Remember that minutes and seconds are in 60ths, so if something is X degrees, Y minutes, and Z seconds, the decimal equivalent is $X + Y/60 + Z/3600$.

So let's add your new tags to your web site in the next section.

Configuring Meta GeoTags

You can go to the GEOTags.com web site to get the following Meta tags to add to the <head> section of your web page:

<meta name="ICBM" content="**XXX.XXXXX, XXX.XXXXX**">
<meta name="DC.title" content="**THE NAME OF YOUR SITE**">

<meta name="ICBM" content="45.544222, -122.710748">
<meta name="DC.title" content="Orlando Office Stuff">

NOTE: *If your site uses frames, you must add the Meta tags to your **top-level** page which contains the <frameset> tag.*

You can also index *http://www.geotags.com* style "geo.position" Meta tag as per their documentation at: *http://geotags.com/geobot/add-tags.html*

The reason it is called the ICBM address is that this was actually used for generating geographically-correct maps. This became known as one's ICBM address or missile address, and some people include it in their sig block with that name.

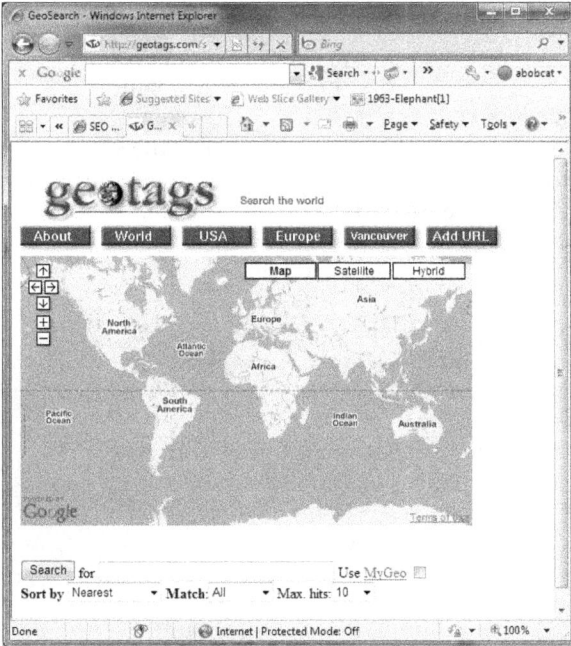

Figure 2.14

So here is what my completed Meta tags should look like in my code of my imaginary furniture store's landing page:

```
<HEAD>
<base href="http://www.Orlandoofficestuff.com/" />
<Title>Orlando Office Furniture | Orlando Office Interiors |
Orlando Office Cubicles </Title>
<Meta http-equiv="Content-type" content="text/html; charset=ISO-
8859-1">
<Meta name="keywords" content="Orlando office furniture,
Orlando office interiors, Orlando office.">
<Meta name="description" content=" Orlando Office Stuff is the
premier source for Orlando office furniture, Orlando office
Interiors, and Orlando office cubicles. We service Orlando,
Gresham, and surrounding areas. We specialize in planning and
outfitting your office environment from top to bottom.">
<Meta name="googlebot" content="index, follow" />
<Meta name="robots" content=" index,follow ">
<Meta name="Revist-After" content="7 days">
<Meta name="city" content="Orlando">
<Meta name="country" content="United States (USA)">
<Meta name="state" content="OR">
<Meta name="zip code" content="97210">
<Meta name="subject" content="Orlando Office Furniture">
<Meta name="author" content="Jason McCormick">
<Meta name="copyright" content="Orlando Office Stuff">
<meta name="geo.region" content="US-OR" />
<meta name="geo.placename" content="Orlando, OR" />
<meta name="ICBM" content="45.544222, -122.710748">
<meta name="DC.title" content="Orlando Office Stuff">
</HEAD
```

Chapter 3 - Submitting Your Web Site to the Search Engines

Let's assume that you, as most people, had a web developer design this completely awesome site but he or she who designed the site didn't have a clue about SEO. Some of my customers have spent thirty thousand dollars on a web site and it didn't even have a single Meta tag on it!

We already talked about matching the title, Meta tags, Meta descriptions, Meta Keywords to the root pages of your web site and having all the same appear in all those areas, right? If you didn't catch that and you are about to submit your website(s) please go back to the last chapter!

If you are done with that, then you are ready to go to the next step!

First Stop, Google.

Why Google? Well, about sixty percent of all web searches happen right on Google, which means that although there are other major search engines, you want to make Google happy first. (I will include a step later where you go to http://www.websitesubmitter.org and submit your web site to the 200+ little search engines for about $35.00. This will save you about 100 hours of your precious time, if not more.)

First off, you will want to go to Google and create a Google account for Google Webmasters.

Step 1 - Add Your Site to Google Webmaster Central

Google's Webmaster Central (as shown in Figure 3.1 below) can be used to notify Google of the existence of a web site, verify with Google that you have control of the web site (Webmaster), identify the site map location for a web site, access keyword research tools, verify the Robot.txt file, and locate any errors within a web site.

To add your web site to the Google Webmaster Central, do the following:

1. Go to http://www.google.com/services as shown in Figure 3.1. Then click on the Webmaster Central Link.

2. After you have created the account you should be able to access Google Webmaster tools. Right in the middle of the page should be an icon that says, "Add site".

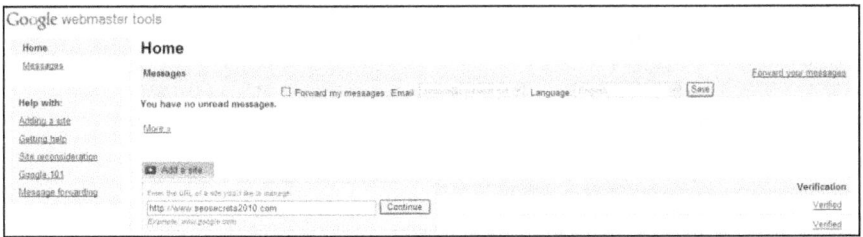

Figure 3.1

3. You can then place a Meta tag which Google gives you on your web site or upload an HTML file. This is used to verify that you truly are the webmaster. Once Google confirms it has verified your web site URL, the next stop is Google Analytics.

   NOTE: *Later we will add a Google Sitemap.xls to the web site to help Google index all of your pages.*

Step 2 - Add your site to Google Analytics

1. Go to http://www.google.com/services as shown in Figure 3.2 below. Then click on the Analytics link. You should already be logged in but if not, log in using the same account you used for the Google Webmaster Central.

2. After you have accessed Google Analytics, again right in the middle of the page should be an icon that says, "Add New Profile".

3. Then add the web site URL as shown below and click Finish:

Figure 3.2

> **NOTE:** *If you want your business to be seen in the Local Business Results on Google, see Google Local Business Listings and Bing Local Business Listings in the next chapter.*

Step 3 - Submitting your site to Yahoo!

At the time of this writing, you can still submit your web site for free to Yahoo.com at: http://siteexplorer.search.yahoo.com/submit. But that is expected to change as Yahoo is now going to get its results from Bing.com.

Submitting your site for free to Yahoo! (as shown in Figure 3.3):

1. Create a Yahoo! ID at http://www.yahoo.com
2. Go to: http://siteexplorer.search.yahoo.com/submit
3. Enter the web site URL and press Submit URL as shown below.

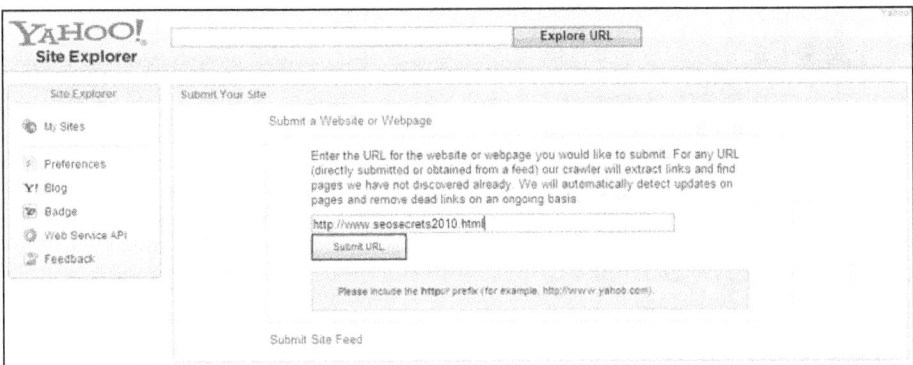

Figure 3.3

Step 4 - Submitting your site to Bing

Bing.com is gaining an incredible market share—especially since they are owned by Microsoft and the engine is used to perform searches not only on Bing, but on MSN, Live, and many other smaller sites. And guess what? Now, some Yahoo! results as well as a deal was made to allow Bing to provide the results and advertising on Yahoo! as well.

To submit your web site to Bing.com, follow these instructions:

1. Go to the URL of: http://www.bing.com/docs/submit.aspx as shown in Figure 3.4.

Figure 3.4

2. Enter the verification characters.

3. Enter the URL of the web site you want to submit to Bing.com and then click "Submit URL".

4. You get a message thanking you for submitting your site to Bing as shown below in Figure 3.5:

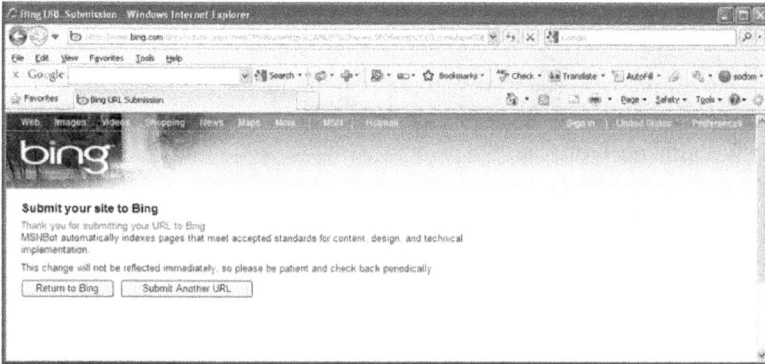

Figure 3.5

Bing's Webmaster Center

Bing's Webmaster Center, as shown below, can be used to notify Bing of the existence of a web site, verify with Bing that you have control of the web site (Webmaster), identify the site map location for a web site, access keyword research tools, verify the Robot.txt file, and locate any errors with a web site.

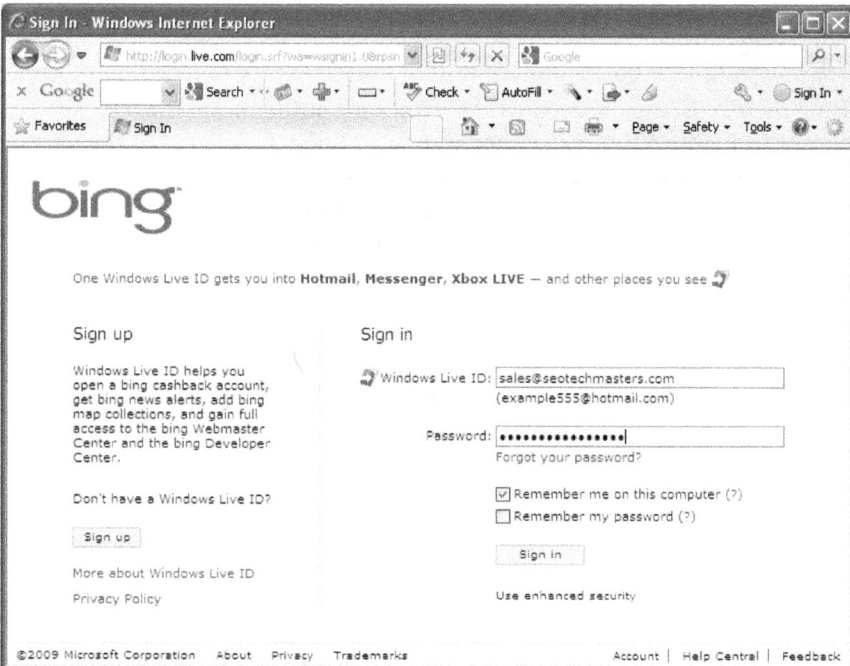

Figure 3.6

The Bing webmaster console as shown above can be found at:

http://www.bing.com/webmaster/WebmasterManageSitesPage.as px

In Figure 3.6 above, you see that you are logging in. Since I have a new client who is an author of travel guides, let's add their newest web site to the Bing Webmaster Console.

In Figure 3.7 you will notice that I have added their web site address, the address of the site map I have created, and the email address. Since I do their SEO services, I enter my email address as the Webmaster's email.

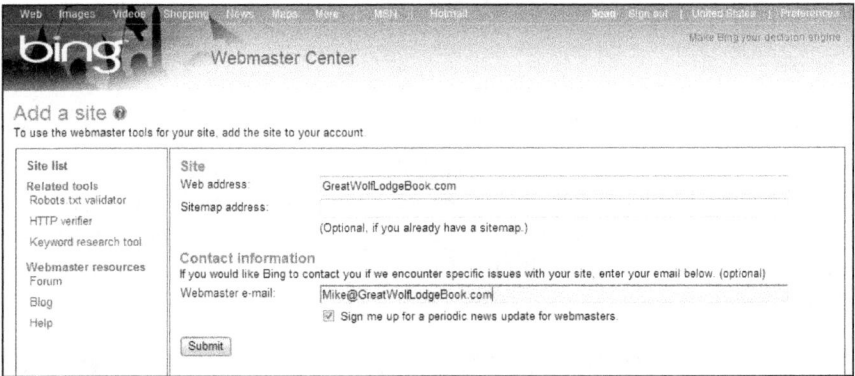

Figure 3.7

Bing then gives me a screen which makes me authenticate the web site, as shown in Figure 3.8. I can either add an additional Meta tag to the tags I have created or upload a verification file to the web site to verify that I am the owner or webmaster of the web site. I usually download the file as you never know what will happen to the landing page of the web site in the future.

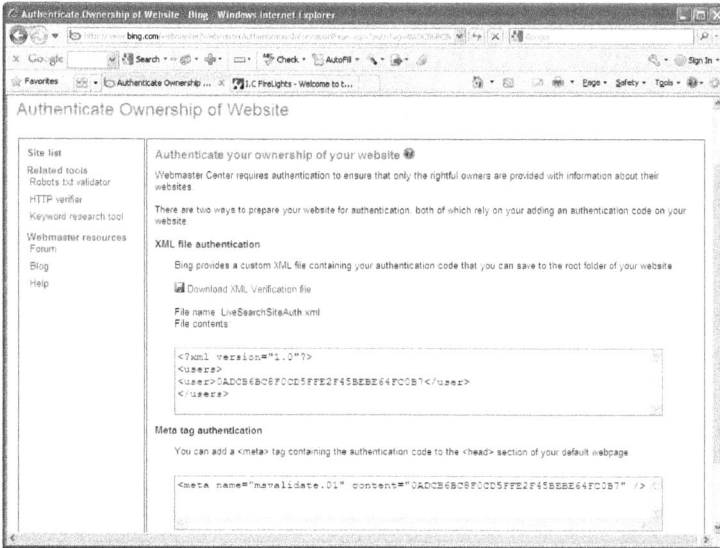

Figure 3.8

In Figure 3.9, you will see the web site amongst other web sites I have verified. It shows the web site name and on the right it shows how I authenticated the web site. The middle characters are the verification code assigned by Bing.com.

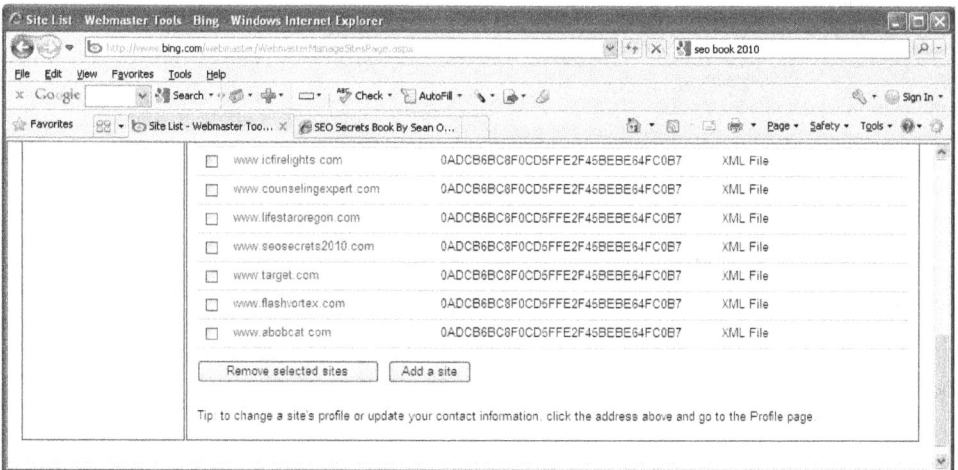

Figure 3.9

Step 5 - Submitting to DMOZ

DMOZ (also known as the Open Directory Project), as shown in Figure 3.10, is important because AOL Search, AltaVista, HotBot, Lycos, and Netscape Search all increase the ranking of your site if they are listed there. Follow these rules and instructions for submitting your site there:

1. Go to http://www.dmoz.org
2. First find the category that best fits your web site.
3. Choose "Suggest URL" in the top right corner. If it is not available it means that there are more subcategories and you need to drill down and choose the one that best fits your business.
4. Add the Site URL, title and description as shown below. Then select submit at the bottom of the page.

Figure 3.10

DMOZ has certain rules to follow, as seen on their web site:

- Do not add mirror sites.
- Do not submit an URL that contains only the same or similar content as other sites you may have listed in the directory. Multiple submissions of the same or related sites may result in the exclusion and/or deletion of those and all affiliated sites.
- Do not disguise your submission and submit the same URL more than once.

  Example: http://www.dmoz.org and http://www.dmoz.org/index.html.
- Do not submit any site with an address that redirects to another address.
- The Open Directory has a policy against the inclusion of sites with illegal content. Examples of illegal material include child pornography; libel; material that infringes any intellectual property right; and material that specifically advocates, solicits or abets illegal activity (such as fraud or violence).
- Do not submit sites "under construction."
- Submit pornographic sites to the appropriate category under Adult.
- Submit non-English sites to the appropriate category under World.
- Don't submit sites consisting largely of affiliate links.

Violating any of these rules can get your URL removed or not listed at all.

Step 6 - Submitting to Alexa

Submitting your web site to Alexa is important as this is another site that helps demonstrate your web site's importance to major search engines. To add your web site, do the following:

1. Submit to Alexa as shown in Figure 3.11 has a lot of weight to Google and other search engines.

2. First go to http://www.alexa.com/edit

3. Once you submit the URL it will give you the option to update the URL information as shown below.

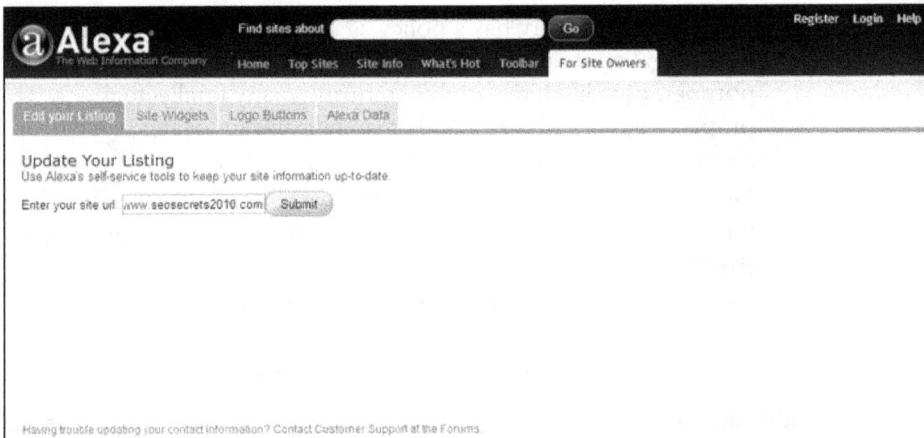

Figure 3.11

4. After you have completed the entry it will give you two options to verify the information: It can either e-mail you a confirmation or give you an info.txt file to place at the root of your web sites FTP folder.

5. Once you have entered an e-mail or uploaded the info.txt file, press one of the confirmation link buttons.

Step 7 - Submitting to AllCanSee

Adding your site to AllCanSee.com (as shown in Figure 3.12) couldn't be easier. To add your web site to AllCanSee.com, do the following:

1. First go to this URL: http://www.allcanseek.com/add

2. Enter a verifiable e-mail address.

3. Enter your sites URL and press submit as shown in the picture below:

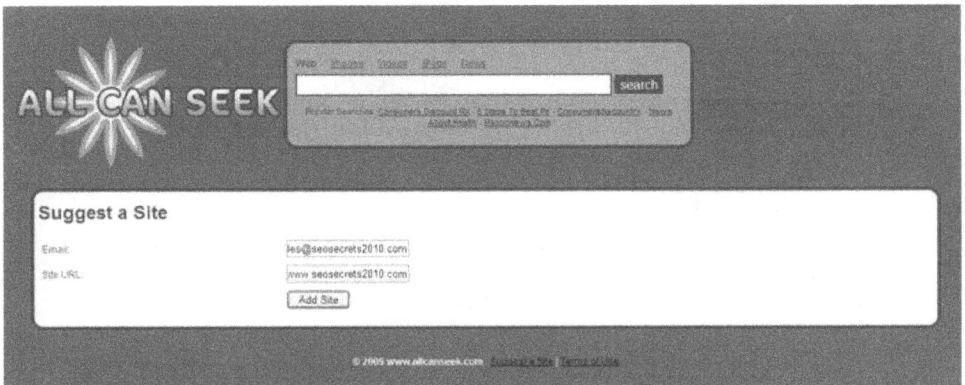

Figure 3.12

Step 8 - Submitting to CanLinks

CanLinks.com creates categorical links to your web site. Google and other web sites then crawl these links and give additional relevance to your site's rankings for your key words.

1. First go to the URL of: http://www.canlinks.net/addalink

CANLINKS Main :: ADDALINK

Now, *Sean Odom*, please Click On Your Link (new window will open): http://www.seosecrets2010.com and review the information for accuracy (close new window to return here) or Go Back to Correct. Then, Click the Final Submission to Canlinks button to complete your submission.

Figure 3.13

2. Enter your name, the name of the site, description, and choose up to six boxes which closely match your web site type. Then press continue.
3. The next page you see should allow you to do a final submission after you verify or edit the information you have provided.

Step 9 - Submitting To Jayde for Business To Business Web sites

Jayde is a specialized search engine catering to businesses only. To add your web site to Jayde, do the following:

1. Go to the URL of: http://submit2.jayde.com/

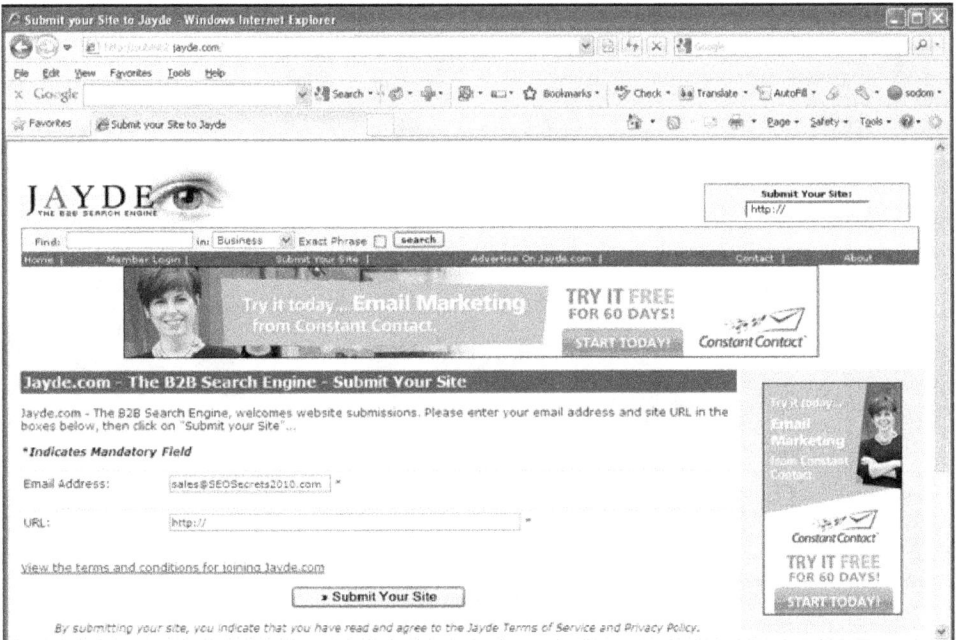

Figure 3.14

2. Enter your email address.

3. Enter the URL you are submitting and press Submit your site.

4. It should return with a message:

"Thank you for submitting to our directory"

Step 10 - Submitting To the Librarians Internet Index (LII)

The Librarians Internet Index is absolutely important to rankings on the major search engines. To add your web site to the Librarians Internet Index, do the following:

1. Go to the URL of shown in Figure 3.15:
   http://lii.org/cs/lii/create/todo

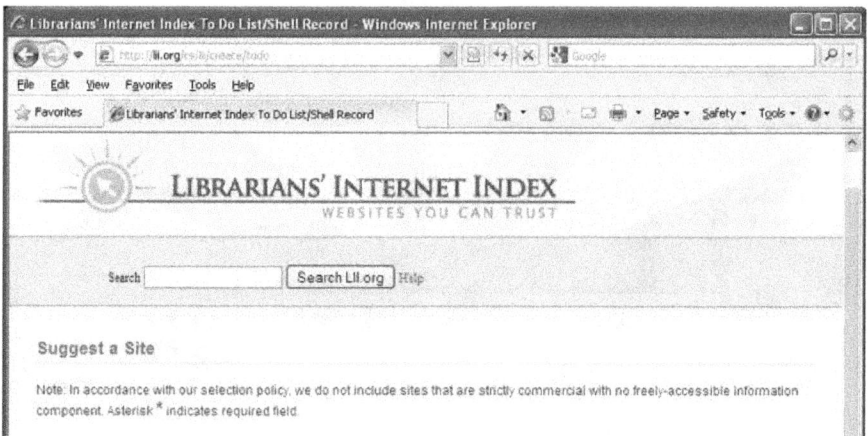

Figure 3.15

2. Enter your name.

3. Enter your email address.

4. Enter the URL you are submitting.

5. Enter a short description of your web site.

6. Enter a comment or a more in-depth description.

7. Enter the verification characters and press "Submit"

You will get a confirmation email that suggests registering your web site through their contact form as well, which I highly recommend.

They do have some criteria for what types of sites can be listed. You can find the criteria here: http://lii.org/pub/htdocs/selectioncriteria.htm

Step 11 - Enlisting your URL and company on Merchant Circle

Merchant Circle (as shown in Figure 3.16) is one of those web sites that didn't seem like much when it first started but then caught on quickly. If you have a web presence on the web you should join and list your business there. It creates a link to your web site as well as generates local and national advertising for your business.

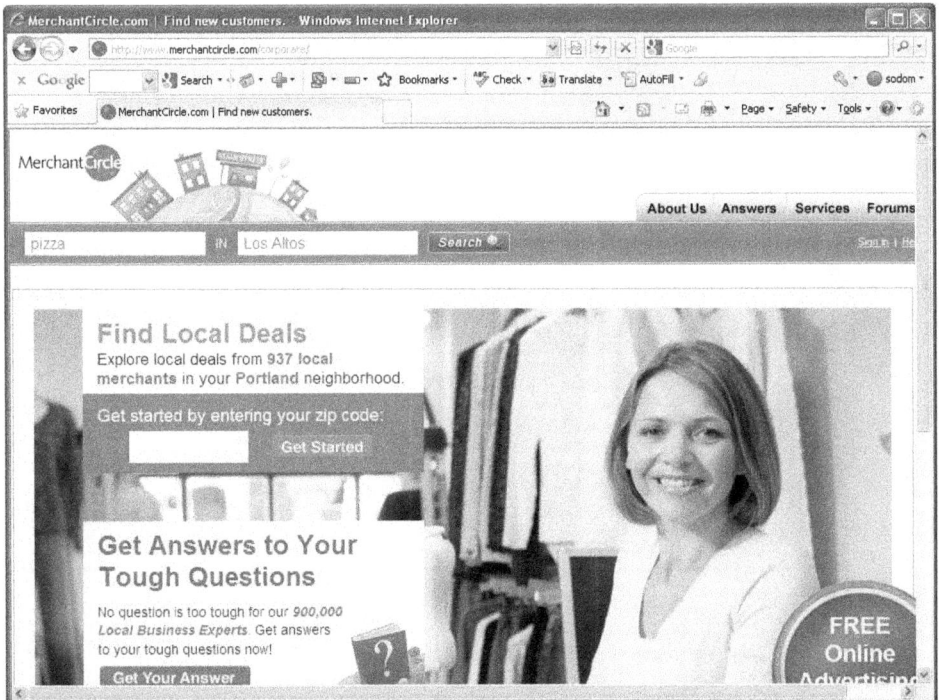

Figure 3.16

Step 12 - Enlist your URL on WhatUSeek

WhatUSeek.com is a search engine used by businesses on the Internet. To add your web site to WhatUSeek.com, do the following:

1. Go to the URL of: http://www.whatuseek.com/addurl-secondary.shtml

Figure 3.17

2. Enter your web sites URL.

3. Enter your email address, check the appropriate boxes, and press submit URL.

   NOTE: *Listing your company is free. However, the next screen will give you paid options which are not required.*

Step 13 - Submitting To National Directory

National Directory (as shown in Figure 3.18) is a directory, not a search engine. To add your web site, do the following:

1. Go to the URL of:
   http://www.nationaldirectory.com/submit.php

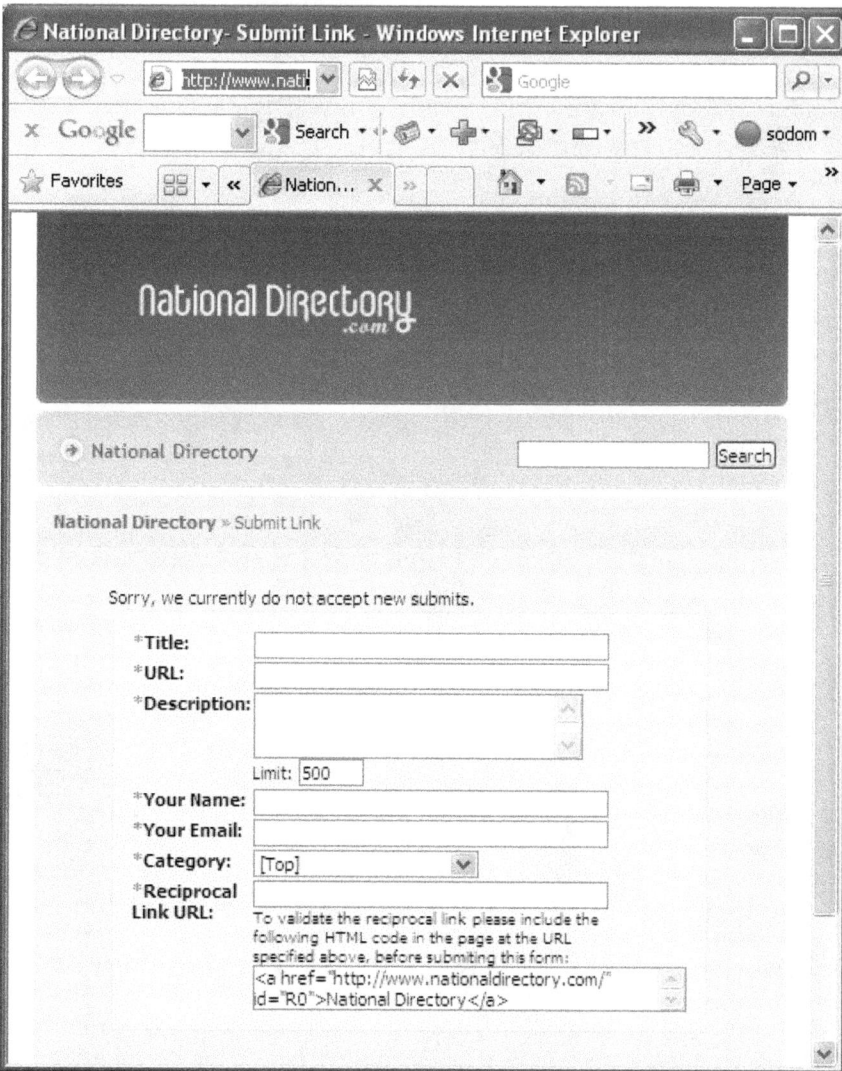

Figure 3.18

2. Add your title.

3. Add your web site's URL.
4. Add a description that includes at least the first three keywords in your keyword's Meta tag.
5. Add your name and email address.
6. Select the category of your business.
7. Add the URL of the webpage. You will enter the tag information they give you below to verify your ownership of the web site.

Step 14 – Using Web site Submission Engine to Make the Rest of the Job Easy

There are hundreds of other smaller search engines and directories, as well as major search engines for other countries. You never know when someone is going to use one of these smaller search engines; since you are competing with a lower number of sites, your chances are higher that the smaller number of users will find your web site a greater percentage of the time.

You might have Figured out that getting your site included in search engines and directories is no easy task. It takes a lot of time, research, and if you don't follow all the directions to the letter, you risk the chance of being refused for listing on web sites.

There are submission web sites which use custom tools that are automated software programs and applications that remember the repetitive information that must be provided in order to get your web site listed in hundreds of search engine and directories.

Many submission tools try to scam web site owners by promising to submit their site to thousands of search engines and directories for one low fee. The problem with that claim is that most of those search engines are either nonexistent or mostly worthless to your site.

You absolutely need help in submitting your web site to the smaller search engines and directories as there are hundreds of them. It would take you months to add your site to every one of these sites on your own. However, for about $15.95 you can have a company that specializes in submitting web sites do it instantly.

We highly recommend the Submission Complete (as shown in Figure 3.19) at http://www.submisssioncomplete. It's the engine that we at Website SEO Professional's use as well as many other SEO companies. They are reputable and always get the job done right.

Figure 3.19

Figure 3.20

There are many packages that you can choose from in Figure 3.20.

If you are doing your own *search engine optimization*, the bigger the package you get, the less you have to do on your own. In fact the high end packages actually help you decide your keywords, create your Meta tags, and scan your site of optimization problems. Most of the important work is done for you.

If you need professional SEO help you can always

Chapter 4 – Local Business Listings

Local Business Listings help consumers find retail locations. If you have a local business or a business with local store locations you can list those stores in the Local Business Listings on either Google or Bing. Keep in mind that by listing the business on Bing you are listing the business on MSN, Live, and most likely Yahoo as well.

One of the great things about the local listings (as shown in Figures 4.1 and 4.2) is that they automatically appear at the top of the listings. Additionally, your retail location shows on the map that is provided as well.

Let's take a look at the Local Business Listing results for "Orlando pizza" on both Bing and Google, starting with Bing in Figure 4.1.

Figure 4.1

Next, let's look at the same search on Google in Figure 4.2.

Figure 4.2

They are very similar. Again, there are some differences. Google usually wants to see relevance to the search term (in this case, "Orlando pizza.") Bing not only wants to see relevance but also that your address is the closest to Orlando, Florida. If your business is in Oregon City and you come up first in the organic listings for the search term, "Orlando pizza," you did a great job optimizing your web site and making it relevant to the search term.

On the other hand, your business's physical address is not in Orlando, so other companies that are in Orlando or very close to Orlando will show up on Bing's Local Business listings before your company does.

There is also one other factor that helps in this situation. Each listing allows you to click on it and get more information on both Google and Bing Local Business listings. Each gives you the ability to see more information on the business and give reviews. These reviews give some weight to whom is shown on the listings.

A good recommendation is to encourage your customers (via email or some other advertising form) to leave positive reviews if they like your product or services. Both Google and Bing are pretty good at identifying false reviews, especially if you leave more than one from the same login or IP address.

So let's take a look at adding your business to the Local Business listings of both Google and Bing, starting with Bing, in the following sections.

Adding a Local Business Listing to Bing

First off, you need to know where to go. For Bing, the Local Business listings are added at the Local Listing Center (as shown in Figure 4.3) at the following address:

https://ssl.bing.com/listings/ListingCenter.aspx

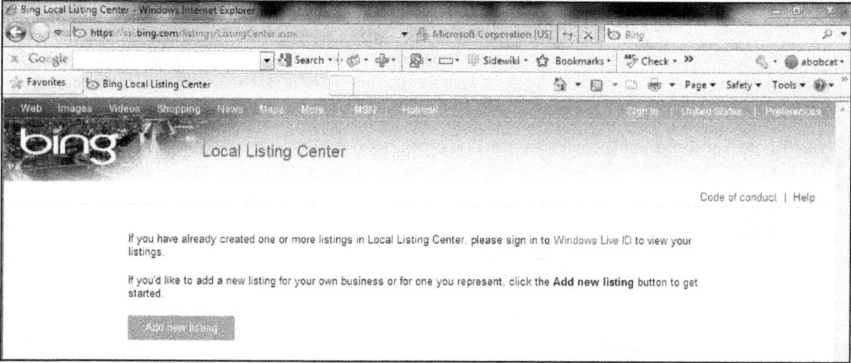

Figure 4.3

I can go ahead and add a new listing and create a login. I already have a login, so I will login and it will immediately show my current listings, as shown in Figure 4.4.

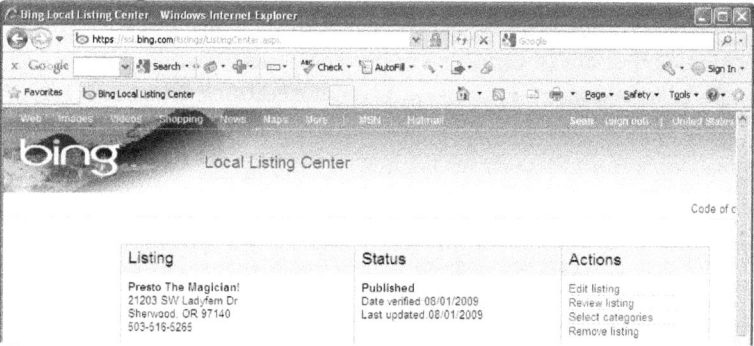

Figure 4.4

Let's return to the website ICFireLights. I will use them as an example and add them by clicking Add New Listing to the Bing Local Listings Center (starting in Figure 4.5). (All this information is public information, so there is no confidential information here.)

Figure 4.5

You will notice I only added the required name and email address to get started. They don't have a public address, so that was not shown on the screen. I also checked the option to not display the address on the Local Listing. The next screen I get (as shown in Figure 4.6) is the hours of operation. Since they sell online 24 hours a day, I selected the first option, stating that they are "Open 24 hours a day". I also clicked on all the forms of payment that their web site is willing to take by checking each option.

Figure 4.6

The next screen you get (as shown in Figure 4.7) allows you to enter the year they were established, a tagline, a business description, brands carried, and any specialty items or services the business provides.

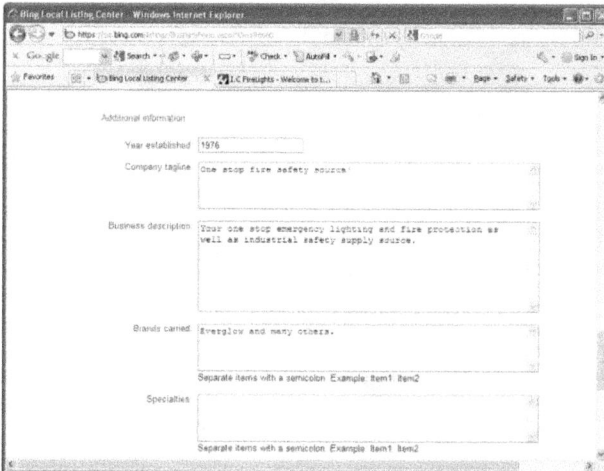

Figure 4.7

The next screen (as shown in Figure 4.8) allows you to choose the predefined categories that your business falls under. You can choose up to six. Choose what fits your company best based on the keywords you came up with in Chapter 2.

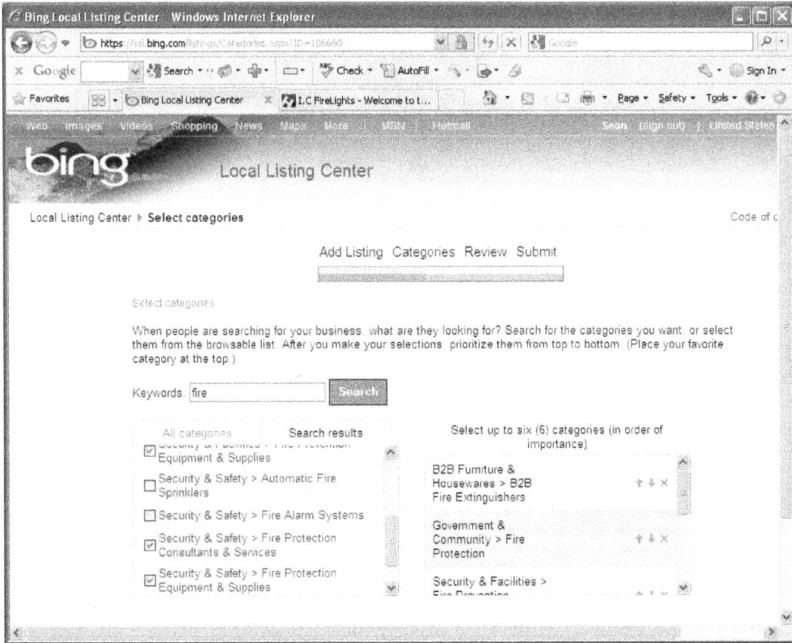

Figure 4.8

Once you have entered all the information in the previous screens, Bing puts all the information together to let you verify it, as shown in Figure 4.9.

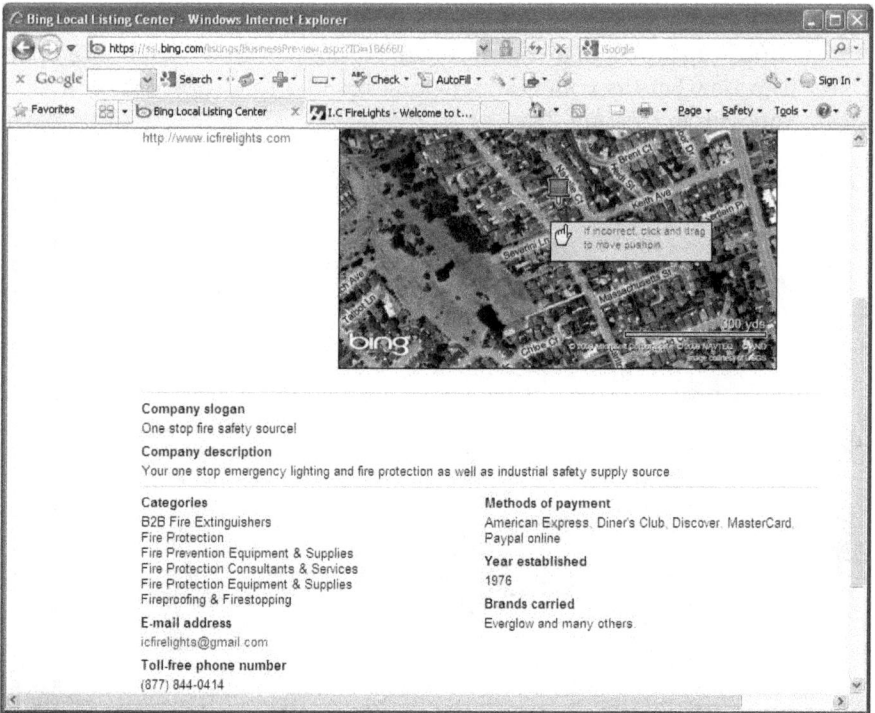

Figure 4.9

The next step is to verify that your business really is at the location you specified. Bing will send you a postcard with a pin number to the address you entered. When you come back to the listings (as shown in Figure 4.4 a few pages back), the Status column allows you to enter the pin number from the card when it arrives in the mail, as shown in Figure 4.10.

Figure 4.10

Adding a Local Business Listing To Google

First off, you need to know where to go. For Google, the local business listings are added at the Local Business Center (as shown in Figure 4.11) at the following address:

http://www.google.com/local/add

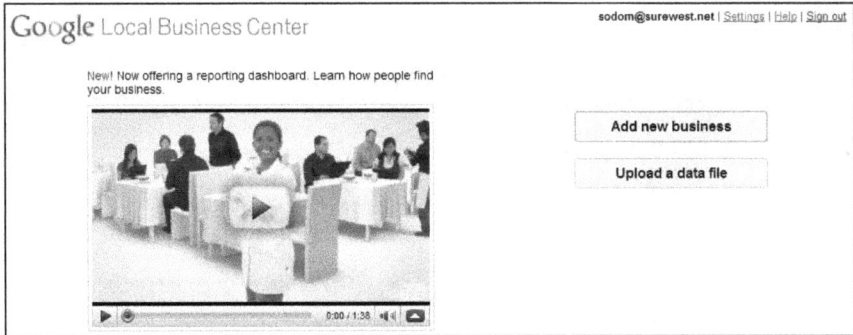

Figure 4.11

If you are already logged in to Google and you have been here before, it will list all your current business listings as shown in Figure 4.12.

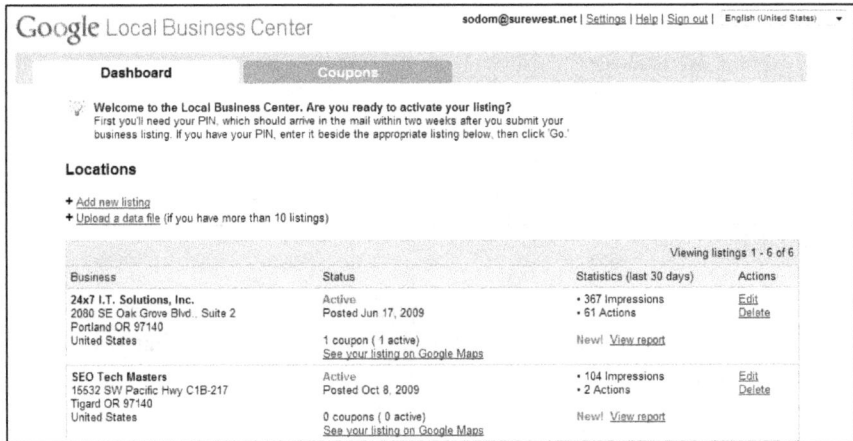

Figure 4.12

You will notice from Figure 4.12 that there are a few more options than on Bing's version. Also, you see how many times your business was shown on the listings and how many people clicked on it. Only recent information is shown. Notice the option to "View Report." This will show you legacy information and give you a more accurate view.

Since we are focused on adding your business, let's click on the Add New Listing option and begin as shown in Figure 4.13 and 4.14 (I had to make it two Figures because the screen was so large).

Figure 4.13

Figure 4.14

The next screen you see appears in Figure 4.15 below. This screen allows you to enter the hours of operation and the payment types that your business accepts, as shown below.

▾ **Hours of operations**

Make sure your customers know when you're open!

○ I prefer not to specify operating hours.
◉ My operating hours are:

Mon:	9:00 AM ▾	- 5:00 PM ▾	☐ Closed	⇩ Apply to all
Tue:	9:00 AM ▾	- 5:00 PM ▾	☐ Closed	
Wed:	9:00 AM ▾	- 5:00 PM ▾	☐ Closed	
Thu:	9:00 AM ▾	- 5:00 PM ▾	☐ Closed	
Fri:	9:00 AM ▾	- 5:00 PM ▾	☐ Closed	
Sat:			☑ **Closed**	
Sun:			☑ **Closed**	

Are your hours split during a single day, such as 9-11am *and* 7-10pm?
☐ I'd like to enter two sets of hours for a single day.

▾ **Payment options**

Specify how customers can pay at your business.

☑ Cash	☑ American Express	☐ Visa
☑ Check	☑ Diner's Club	☐ Financing
☐ Traveler's Check	☐ Discover	☐ Google Checkout
☐ Invoice	☑ MasterCard	☑ Paypal

Figure 4.15

The next screen allows you to add a logo, picture, and even video describing your business, as shown in Figure 4.16.

Figure 4.16

Lastly, in Figure 4.17 you have the option to add brands you carry and other details about your business.

Figure 4.17

The last screen (as shown in Figure 4.18) sums up all the information you have entered. You will see in the Figure another customer of mine, Local News Day's information on Google Local Business Listings.

Local News Day

15532 SW Pacific Hwy
C1B-217
Tigard OR 97224
United States

(503) 343-4887
http://www.localnewsday.com

Fix incorrect marker location

Email address:	newsdesk@localnewsday.com
Description:	Portlands Alternative newspaper with classifiedm entertainment reviews, better business listings, and much more.
Payment types:	Check, American Express, Cash, Diner's Club, MasterCard, Paypal
Hours:	Monday: 9:00 am - 5:00 pm
	Tuesday: 9:00 am - 5:00 pm
	Wednesday: 9:00 am - 5:00 pm
	Thursday: 9:00 am - 5:00 pm
	Friday: 9:00 am - 5:00 pm
	Saturday: Closed
	Sunday: Closed

Figure 4.18

The last thing you have to do is choose how you want Google to verify your business. There are two options (as shown below in Figure 4.19) which are:

1.   Google can verify the phone number by calling you and giving you a pin number over the phone.

101

2.   The other way, Google can verify the address by sending you a pin number by mail.

Google Local Business Center

How would you like to validate your listing?
For your protection, we need to verify the information you've just given us. This can be done one of 2 ways:

- **By phone**
  We'll call you at this phone number (503) 692-9082
- **By postcard (2-3 weeks)**
  We'll send you a postcard in the mail to this address

Figure 4.19

Verifying by phone is the quickest option, but if you choose this, have the phone sitting right next to you because they often call in less than 10 seconds to give you your pin number. Enter this number on the main listing screen, which lists all the businesses you have listed on the Google Business Listings (as shown in Figure 4.20).

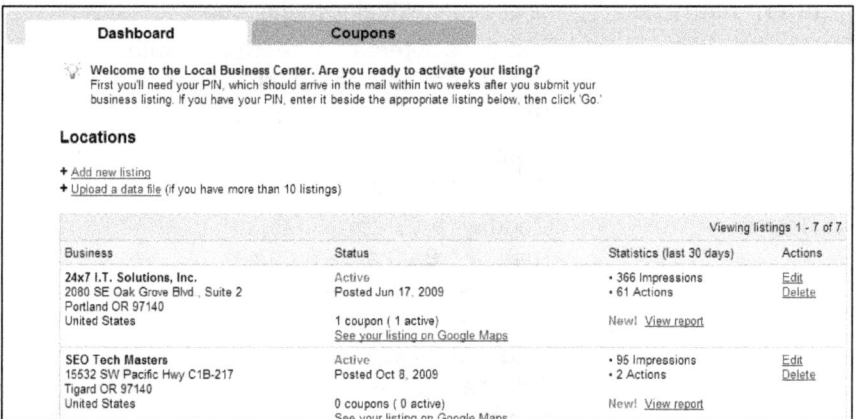

Dashboard	Coupons

Welcome to the Local Business Center. Are you ready to activate your listing?
First you'll need your PIN, which should arrive in the mail within two weeks after you submit your business listing. If you have your PIN, enter it beside the appropriate listing below, then click 'Go.'

Locations

+ Add new listing
+ Upload a data file (if you have more than 10 listings)

Viewing listings 1 - 7 of 7

Business	Status	Statistics (last 30 days)	Actions
24x7 I.T. Solutions, Inc. 2080 SE Oak Grove Blvd , Suite 2 Portland OR 97140 United States	Active Posted Jun 17, 2009 1 coupon (1 active) See your listing on Google Maps	• 366 Impressions • 61 Actions New! View report	Edit Delete
SEO Tech Masters 15532 SW Pacific Hwy C1B-217 Tigard OR 97140 United States	Active Posted Oct 8, 2009 0 coupons (0 active) See your listing on Google Maps	• 95 Impressions • 2 Actions New! View report	Edit Delete

Figure 4.20

One more really interesting thing you can do in the Google Business Listings is offer coupons. If someone clicks on your local business link next to the map on searches you can offer them a coupon. Once your business is verified, click on the Coupons Tab and choose "Add new coupon," as shown below in Figure 4.21. (This shows a coupon offer I have already entered for a Free Network Analysis from one of my SEO customers.)

| Dashboard | | Coupons | | |

Coupons

+ Add new coupon

Coupon offer	Status	Valid at locations	Actions
Free Network Analysis And Security Act Risk Assessment	Active Never Expires	**1 location:** 24x7 I.T. Solutions, Inc. 2080 SE Oak Grove Blvd., Suite 2 Portland OR 97140 United States	Edit - Pause - Delete - Link New

Figure 4.21

So let's sum up this chapter. You entered your local business listings with Bing.com and with Google. You learned how to increase your relevance by having customers give good reviews of your business, how to verify your company information so you can start being listed in both search engines' Local Business Listings, and how to add coupons to your listings in Google.

Now let's take a look at another important optimization technique which helps to increase your rankings by linking other web site pages to your own web site in the next chapter.

Adding Your Local Listing To Yahoo!

Yahoo is still in the top 3 search engines and with their partnership with Bing.com, you can bet their share of the search engine market will only grow. Here are the instructions to add your website to the local business listings of Yahoo!.

1. Go to local listing to add your business at the following URL as shown in Figure 4.22:

   http://listings.local.yahoo.com/csubmit/index.php

Figure 4.22

2. Enter in all your pertinent information for your business including your business hours, phone numbers, and the types of payments you take as shown in Figure 4.23.

Categories:
Here are the categories we think this business belongs to. Did we get it right? Click the trash icon to delete a category.

☐ Internet Marketing
☐ Marketing Agencies
☐ Web Services

add new category

▽ Additional Information

Toll-Free Phone: **Fax:**
                              503-926-9116

Additional Phone Numbers:

Company Email:
sales@seotechmasters.com

Hours of Operation

○ Do not display operating hours
○ 24 hours a day
◉ Use hours of operation below:

Additional Hours of Operation:

Monday:	Tuesday:	Wednesday:	Thursday:	Friday:	Saturday:	Sunday:
9:00 a.m. ▼	9:00 a.m. ▼	9:00 a.m. ▼	9:00 a.m. ▼	9:00 a.m. ▼	Closed ▼	Closed ▼
to	to	to	to	to	to	to
5:00 p.m. ▼	5:00 p.m. ▼	5:00 p.m. ▼	5:00 p.m. ▼	5:00 p.m. ▼	Closed ▼	Closed ▼

Payment Methods Accepted

☐ Cash Only
☑ Visa
☑ Mastercard
☑ American Express

☐ Discover
☐ Diners Club
☑ Debit Card
☑ Personal Checks

Figure 4.23

3. After you have completed entering all your information including the year and history and verification information press submit and you are done as shown in Figure 4.24.

Additional Information

Year Established
2001
Languages Spoken:
English
Brands Offered:

Products & Services:
SEO, PPC, and SEM marketing.
Professional Associations:
Google Ambassador & SEM PDX
Specialties:

Verify Your Submission
*Enter the code shown:
JyMV24   More Info
This helps Yahoo! prevent automated submissions.

JyMV24

Submit   Reset

Figure 4.24

Other Local Listing Sites

Ask City™ http://national.citysearch.com/guide	**To Add Edit Delete listings on AskCity.** They gets editorial and user reviews from a variety of sites around the web including **CitySearch, Yelp.com and Insiderpages**.
Windows Live Local powered by **Virtual Earth** http://webapp.localeze.com/extranet/login.aspx	**Business listings for the US to Add Edit Delete go there. Microsoft Live Local,** an online local search and mapping service that combines unique bird's-eye imagery with advanced driving directions, **Yellow Pages** and other local search tools.
TrueLocal http://www.truelocal.com/listabusiness.aspx	**To Add Edit Delete a listing. TrueLocal** is a **local search engine** free to hundreds of thousands of users. It is an Internet business directory with brains because you can **full text search** on it.
Local.com BETA™ https://advertise.local.com/	**To Add Edit Delete a listing** Local.com, launched in August 2005, is a **local search engine** owned and operated by Interchange Corporation. Powered by the company's proprietary Keyword DNA and **local Web indexing technologies,** Local.com enables consumers to find **local businesses, products and services.** Local.com's Advertiser network includes **Citysearch, Verizon SuperPages.com and Yahoo**!. to Local.com.
AOL local BETA powered by **MAPQUEST** http://www.mapquest.com	**To Add Edit Delete a listing** powered by mapquest and core data provided by infoUSA - AOL Local Search provides access to relevant information specific to your region. Find local businesses, breaking news and other information for your area.
YP.com http://listings.yellowpages.com/	YellowPages.com and YP.com registration is the digital version of the Yellow Pages.

Chapter 5 – Social Media

Social Media is the new billboard of the world. The virtual coffee house where you can go for conversation. If your company is not in social media for letting consumers know about products or services it provides, then your company better be there for better rankings.

Google Caffeine which is the new indexing platform for Google looks at Social Media to see how well you market your products or services and uses that information as part of its decision factors of your websites rankings and placement of your website in its organic listings.

In this chapter I am going to cover a lot of ground. I will look at the three social media goals which are unrelated to rankings, I will look at the proper copywriting techniques, the do's and don'ts of social media and using proper etiquette. I will also touch on the top social media websites and who they are and where to go to find them.

It's a lot of ground to cover so let's get started.

Three Primary Social Media Goals

Here I'm going to map out the three primary goals most social media outreach campaigns fall into. If you're still trying to figure out how and why to get involved in social media outreach, consider these three categories and ask yourself how they might apply to your business as shown in Figure 5.1.

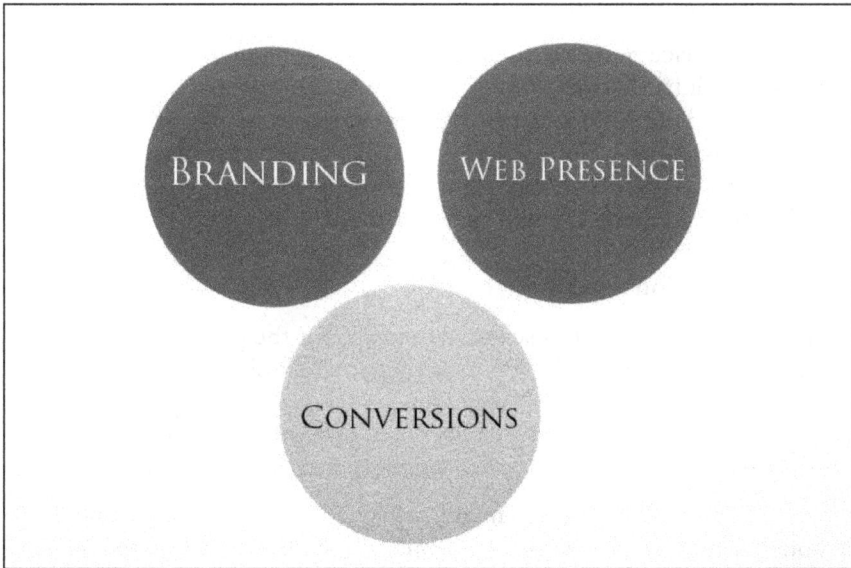

Figure 5.1

When we look at online marketing, there are three broad categories for which nearly all social media related goals can fall in to. They are usually either aimed at:

- Building and Strengthening the Brand
- Driving Conversions
- Increasing and Monitoring your web Presence

Knowing this, let's take a closer look at these three areas and how they might apply to your social media efforts.

Build Your Brand

When it comes to building and reinforcing your brand, social media is one of the most powerful marketing tools available to business owners now. Social Media gives you the strongest and broadest opportunity to both find your target audience and to engage in conversation with them.

These days, you have no choice but to differentiate yourself from your competition. To do this identify the things that make your company different from your competition. This is also known as your Unique Value Proposition(UVP).

If you're a service professional, I recommend that you target a specific niche and build a blogging, Google Buzz and Twitter strategy around that. Demonstrate your expertise in working with a certain type of client and then seek out those types of clients to have conversation with. Look for new ways to connect with them and encourage your current clients to socially share your articles with their networks.

Drive Conversions

One of biggest reasons to use social media is for the potential boost it can have to your conversion efforts. Whether you're looking to drive sales, increase the number of leads your website receives, or simply drive people to an action or a conversions make sure they are easily trackable and there are goals set you want to reach in the realm of social media.

I recommend that you sit down and write out a list of all the potential actions you might want a visitor to your website to take when visiting your company's website.

There are some options that immediately jump out such as choosing to take action to buy your product or services. They may also be to have the customer leave information that you can act on to contact them. Never forget the easy ones either such as to subscribe to your newsletter, referring them to your blog or offering a free product or service white paper.

> When you are done, scan the list you have created and determine the best strategy for effectively obtaining your goals. Plan what social media avenues will be best to use to obtain your goals.

Increase Presence

> The goal most often associated with social media efforts is increasing your web presence and brand recognition by increasing the

conversation level about your product. This can be sparked by a number of things such as news articles, asking questions, responding to questions, and creating topics in social media related to your product and answering how your product fulfills a potential customer's needs.

Using Keyword Density In Social Media

One of the biggest things you can do is learn about keyword density which I explain throughout this book. Whenever you post to a blog, write a news article, or do any tweeting, you should have a keyword in mind. This keyword should be a word that people would type in to a search engine to find the product or service you are advertising in social media.

When you write you should keep a steady 4% keyword density at a minimum. This means that if you post a 200 word blog posting, you should have the keyword in your posting at least 8 times. This will make your posting the most relevant to the search engines for that keyword.

Following this instruction makes social media a prime outlet for PR driven companies who want to know what customers are saying about them and then having those comments found on search engines.

I f you setting up even a baseline (meaning keep track of what happens before your use of social media) will help you to see how well social media is helping your business. Whether you're launching a new product, aiming to get new people to know about your product or service, or target a new audience for your service or products, the potential is unlimited.

When it comes to the conversation people might be having about you online, ask yourself a few questions.

- What demographics do your product or services appeal to?

- What will people be looking for in terms of keywords for your product or services?

- What do you want your clients to be saying about your product or service?

- What can you do to create a buzz or what type of niche does your product or service fulfill better than others?

You've Set the Stage, Now Start Building a Plan

Looking at your business with answers to the questions above will help you set the stage for your social media efforts. If you're small business looking to take your social media efforts up a notch (or maybe even just get started,) take the time to define at least two goals from the questions above. Once you've identified your desired outcome and your target audience, you are ready to start mapping out the path to get there. But how do you write you posts? Let's look at that in the next section.

Social Media Copywriting

No SEO is complete without good writing and this section is more of a tip section than a how to section on good SEO copywriting. Good keyword density in writing is an art that you have to learn and place your keywords in the text so it appears normal to a human visitor reading it.

You can stuff keywords into the text all you want, and that might be okay to get you some decent keyword rankings on search engines but social media has to be appealing to a human visitor and not just a bot, crawler or spider. If you don't sound good and offer legitimate information in good form you can kiss your human following so long. Your chances of long-term success of your business and in social media will be one step closer to having a going out of business sale.

A website and social media without good copywriting is like having the most expensive diamond in the world but nothing to set it in. Attractive content is what you need to drive people to your website and give your visitors the information they need in order for you to make the sale or whatever else you want your website visitors to do.

Understanding Copywriting

To the search engines the content on the page is just a bunch of words. Without making this very complex, the search engine bots, crawlers, and spider analyze the words in social media and then they attempt to determine what each page is about based on the words that are found most on the page.

When a web page covers too many different topics or there is no higher percentage of certain types of keywords, then it makes it difficult for the search engines to determine what topic of the page is. When the focus is diluted search engines tend to either ignore the page or place no relevance on its content. In other words it will be very hard to find on any search engine search.

The search engines have a good idea of how words and topics work together. It's not really about the number of times a keyword is used but the focus of the content now in many circumstances. I like to tell my clients that if you cannot put the content of a blog post in to Microsoft Word and not see a bunch of green underlines meaning the words are not complete sentences. Then you shouldn't post it or put it up on your website. Why? Because search engines use the same technology and know if you are trying to pull the wool over their eyes.

If you use a certain word or phrase too much then it'll be seen as trying to manipulate the search engines. Too little content and it's not enough to be relevant. I recommend that you try to maintain at least 300 words with a 4% keyword density in blog posts.

Write as much or as little text as is needed in order to make the point you need for your visitors but never go below the 300 words.

Get Attention In your Posts

Copywriting isn't all that different from normal copywriting except that you have to pay particular attention to the keywords you want to use. When you write it should not appear as SEO copywriting. At the same time you should use phrases that attract and appeal to the readers not just search engines.

If the reader hits the page and the content is unable to get and keep their focus and attention, then you have failed in your quest. Your initial paragraphs should hold their interest and have a link to your product or service, if not the reader may move on to another page or another site and you have failed at your goal

Make Sure You Meet Their Needs

Once you have the reader's attention then you have to make your case and use clear an precise instructions and suggestions on the best product or service for their need. You also need to tell the reader exactly what they need to do to get your product or service.

Sell them on the product in the post and don't send them to another page where they get more information. Send them to the page to make the sale or enter information for the lead you need. The fewer the clicks the better.

You already have shown them what they want and the answer to their question or their needs. You should know what motivated them to search for what you offer and then clearly re-iterating the need, you are then in a position to show that you have the solution. **Ask questions**

> *TIP: A good technique is to ask a question first and then provide an answer. A question will make your readers consider what they are reading and then seek an answer to the question.*

SIDEBAR: Rules of Copywriting

There are five basic rules to writing good website content that is appealing to both visitors and the search engines.

1. Avoid text in graphics or pictures.

Search engines are not so good about reading text in a graphic format. Some search engines are getting better at it but it is best to avoid graphics or non-standard fonts.

2. Consider your readers before the search engines

Your human readers should come first. The search engines don't buy from you, they add to the comments, and they don't Tweet your message to all their friends if they like you. Only human visitors do that.

3. Write enough content to be accepted.

You need to write enough content to make the points you the human visitor needs.   For the search engines it should never be less than 300 words in a blog post or other posting.

4. Target keyword phrases and not just words.

People rarely search for a single word anymore. They have learned to refine their search to a specific long tail keyword for each of their searches.   What are the ones that apply to your blog, articles, or web page?   You need to know that before you start.   Sometimes the keywords come natural and sometimes you need to go to Google and research keywords. Refer back to Chapter 1 and 2 of this book to learn how to do that.

Social Media Etiquette

Unfortunately, social-media optimization is not as simple as going to a web site and signing up or starting a one paragraph blog and waiting for people to come to your web site. For the most part, they won't.

Approaching social media in that manner will waste your time, and by the time you figure it out the bad reputation you may leave behind may haunt your web site or domain name. Managing your reputation on the web is called *reputation management* in SEO circles and I could write another book just on this topic. I have hundreds of stories on what to look out for and stories of companies ruined on the web because of social media.

The basics to keep yourself from having a bad reputation in social networking is this: when you provide input using social media methods, make sure you do the following:

1. Provide only relative content and no exaggerated claims.
2. Add positive comments and don't make it appear as though you are trying to outdo someone else or are advertising your services. People don't forget when a faker tries to jump in their midst for purely marketing purposes. You are marketing but this is social networking. You are making friends.
3. If you're an expert, make sure your claims are accurate. There are real experts on every subject who will point out your flaws with actual data.
4. Don't ignore people's issues with your product or service. Address them immediately or you are inviting everyone who has ever had a small issue with your product or service to add their two cents.
5. Don't bad mouth a competitor – your only inviting a tidal wave of retribution from your competitor and others.

Seems easy enough, right? Social-media optimization is about first joining communities and creating relationships or friends. It's by going through the process of becoming part of the community and providing relevant and helpful information that your brand will begin to be recognized by other community members. That's when you can announce that your web site has useful information, and your efforts will begin to pay off.

Social Media's Value

Some sites have obvious value in social media. Web sites such as MySpace, Twitter, YouTube, and Facebook are all web sites that no one thought would amount to anything when they began, but they each suddenly took off in their own way, becoming some of the most popular sites on the internet.

Internet users like something to do and to be a part of something bigger. They love to be a part of the community, and that includes online communities as well. The generation that has just entered the workforce and those growing up right now are very computer and internet savvy. For the most part, this generation has been a part of those social networking sites during their schooling. These sites have provided everything from evaluations of teachers, classes, entertainment events, self advertising, keeping up with the latest school rumors, and even schools providing their school event calendars.

When this generation is out of school they become involved in all kinds of activities online, from shopping and downloading music to participating in social networks. The kids are networking socially for different reasons than adults, but both have learned to participate.

Social-Media Strategies

So you have a web site and you need to market it. Using social media is different than most marketing techniques you are taught in economics or marketing in college – At least until they stop using 15-year-old text books. Now there are thousands of sites and you can make your own social media components, but the goals are the same. In the end your goals are to:

- **Know how to target your audience and deliver the right message:** If you approach the wrong audience with the wrong message, you'll learn a quick lesson in reputation management when the court of opinion attempts to destroy your reputation.

- **Create valuable content:** Good content is key to social-media marketing. If you make it a point to create fresh, unique content regularly, visitors will come to you because they know they can find the current information they need. If you're afraid of giving away all your eggs except on a one on one sales call, you will get your message out very slowly.

- **Be a valuable resource, even if it doesn't help you monetarily:** If you try to help without expecting anything in return you gain points and you can gain a good reputation which will, in turn, draw users to your web site. Always wearing your salesman hat works in the corporate world, but online it is a death sentence.

- **Be a user resource:** Internet users, and especially those users who participate in social media and social networking, expect you to provide information that is useful and relevant to them. If you're not providing accurate and helpful information, they'll go to someone who is and bad mouth you on the way.

- **Help your content spread:** One way of advertising your web site's services or products discreetly is to use your trophy and long-tail keywords in your helpful tips and comments on social media sites. Search engines also index this information and when people use search engines to search on those keywords, your blog or other social networking submissions show up. Another good tip is to collect or group your helpful information into other online content such as a PDF, an audio file, or video file which you can provide links for.

- **Increase your linkability:** You want useful information that other site owners find valuable enough to put a link on their web site to yours. The linkability of your site is determined by the amount of content that you have available to users who might come from social networks. Old information that rarely changes will not help, so make sure your content is updated regularly.
- **Make bookmarking your site easy:** Don't make users try to figure out how to add your blog or site to their content feed. Post your URL or code for visitors to add you to their important links or their web site. Use a tool called RSS Button Maker at www.toprankblog.com/tools/rss-buttons to create a button.
- **Reward helpful users:** If you have users that are helpful and/or send business your way, find a way to reward those users so they will continue to be helpful, especially if you made the sale.
- **Don't be afraid to try new things**: Use your creativity to do something different as often as possible. In social-media optimization, creativity is rewarded.

Social media marketing is a great tool if used wisely. It can also be a terrible one if you use it wrong. Using the wrong tactics or using them only half way will render your efforts worthless. You can also expect that it will be very hard to rebuild the trust that you destroy on the web.

There are some rules of etiquette to follow that will help you keep out of trouble. Let's take a look at those in the next section.

Speak To Your Audience

As an SEO expert, I find that companies come to me frequently because their web reputation has been injured, many times unintentionally by their own staff and sometimes through no fault of their own.

Let's take a look at a few rules of etiquette that you should follow to keep yourself from becoming a statistic in the bad category:

1. Spend some time listening to your audience before you join the conversation so you can gain an understanding of the language, the tone, and the expectations of the conversation participants.
2. After you begin to interact with social media elements, use the information that you gather watching and listening on a social networks to ensure that your strategy is targeting the correct people and that the responses to your input are positive.
3. Track your site metrics to see if there are any sudden spikes or dips in your web traffic which could indicate that your involvement is effective or ineffective.
4. Provide only content that adds value to the conversation. If your content doesn't add anything or is inaccurate, the other participants will either ignore you or begin to destroy you.
5. Use RSS feeds. RSS feeds instantly update those who have chosen to watch your content. This means that your links will spread faster than you could ever imagine.
6. Keep in mind that social media is all about relationships. Both engage in and be willing to encourage participation.
7. Make an individual approach as an expert in your service or product. Approaching as the business or company will automatically create suspicion. They may think you are just there to sell something. If you don't have the time yourself, consider hiring bloggers or others to handle your company's social-media participation.

Social Media Outlets

There are many types of social media elements out there in the web world for you to tap into. It is sometimes referred to as Web 2.0 and is definitely the major shift in SEO right now. Web 2.0 is all about the social nature of the internet, and if you don't tap into that social aspect, the SEO on your site will quickly be out-of-date and ranked very low on every major search engine. Using social-media elements, however, you can get a jump-start on your social-media strategy.

So where do you start? Here are some suggestions on what sites you should visit and incorporate into your web site:

- ✓ **Blogger:** www.blogger.com
- ✓ **Blogspot:** www.blogspot.com
- ✓ **Crunchbase:** www.crunchbase.com
- ✓ **Delicious Bookmarks**: www.delicious.com
- ✓ **Digg:** www.digg.com
- ✓ **Furl:** www.furl.net
- ✓ **Twitter:** www.twitter.com
- ✓ **MySpace:** www.myspace.com
- ✓ **Facebook:** www.facebook.com
- ✓ **LinkedIn:** www.linkedin.com
- ✓ **Merchant Circle:** www.merchantcircle.com
- ✓ **Micro Persuasion:** www.micropersuasion.com
- ✓ **Propeller:** www.propeller.com
- ✓ **StumbleUpon:** www.stumbleupon.com
- ✓ **Reddit:** www.reddit.com
- ✓ **Newsvine:** www.newsvine.com
- ✓ **Fark:** www.fark.com
- ✓ **Clipmarks:** www.clipmarks.com
- ✓ **Shoutwire:** www.shoutwire.com
- ✓ **Smogger Social Media Blog:** smogger.wordpress.com
- ✓ **YouTube:** www.youtube.com
- ✓ **Wikipedia:** www.wikipedia.com

These sites each have a different social media element which can be incorporated into your web site. But here is a little tip! In SEO circles the saying goes, "Have more to do with Google and Google will have more to do with you." It couldn't be more true in social media either. Why am I telling you this? Well from that list above, Google owns and runs Blogger.com, Blogspot.com and YouTube.com. So if you're just starting with social media elements, which do you think will give you the greatest rankings on Google? You're right, brain scientist, the ones owned by Google.

Social Media Do's and Don'ts

Here I will outline a lot of principles that are sometime not known right way when approaching social media. Let's first start with the don'ts and then the do's:

DON'T spam-Spamming is over using social media to broadcast the same message over and over with no real change. Sending the same Tweet 5 times an hour is spamming.

DON'T post questionable photos-Especially of others without their permission and in the right setting.

DON'T keep conversations private.-If you're keeping every social interaction private, why are you even taking part in social media? Stick to emails and instant messengers and text messaging if that's your goal, and stop making everyone else feel like your "club" is too exclusive.

DON'T pick on your competitors-If you attack a competitor you become a target. Not just for them but for everyone else. As an SEO Expert my company cleans up the messes every day from a misguided employee or sales person that ties to tear a competitor down by pointing out their flaws. They usually find flaws in you and when attacked the quiet giant tends to invest money and effort attacking you. Usually they one up you and sometimes 10x up you.

Don't try to get someone banned on purpose-I see this a lot, social media sabotage by trying to bury another writers posts or news stories with negative posts, trying to get them banned from social media platforms, or pretending to be an unhappy customer for another companies products. The person who is doing the attack usually gets exposed one way or the other and gets a black eye in the end. Internet users are very smart and they can tell when someone is blatantly trying this approach.

DON'T send automated messages-Don't buy software and automated tools to send out posts. Most users can tell and they hate you. When people see those types of posts they drop following you in a heartbeat.

DON'T create multiple user names to post comments- If other people aren't supporting your point of view or are not interested in what you have to offer, that should give you a clue. It's never okay to comment using multiple fake identities to try to support your own point and your writing style is usually a giveaway.

DON'T invite everyone you know to every social media tool you use-There use to be a lot of multi-level marketing schemes and when someone got involved they used to pester their friends and family to join them. He used to be very annoying and avoided at all costs. If a friend or customer is already networking with you in two or three places, that's enough.

DON'T excessively link to your own site or products- No one cares about your site enough to want to see a link to it in every paragraph. One link will do. You'll be viewed as an advertisement instead of providing good information and for others as a link spammer.

DO think before speaking–This is very important that you preplan your approach with proper keywords. Just because something pops into your head, it doesn't mean it should be shared with the world. Think first because some comments can't be deleted once they are sent.

DO personalized messages—On the internet most people reading your posts will not know you. As an author I point out every time my books and my resume in a few words at the beginning or end of my posts. People like to know who they are getting their information from. Especially if you are a well known in your field of expertise.

DO use your real name whenever possible- When you interact online anonymously, very little holds you accountable for your actions and words and people take everything you say with a grain of salt.

DO comment back-This is interaction 101. Social media is a two-way street. Try to give more than as much as you get.

DO try to make your posts comprehensible-If you are familiar with texting lingo, don't bring it to your posts. Many people are not and they find it offensive when they see it. Not only that, it doesn't sound business like or professional except to a teenager.

Chapter 6-Build Your Web site with SEO in Mind

This is the chapter that some of you will look at and want to cry. Probably because you spent tens of thousands of dollars on this all Flash-based, super cool-looking web site that will do nothing to get you better rankings and make your site seem more relevant to the different search engines.

I often hear similar things from prospective customers when I tell them their old site won't work: "What do you mean? My site looks awesome! It's all flashy and things move here and there. It's awesome!"

Well, this is a true story.   Last night before I started working on this chapter I met with a new client who is starting his own business doing psychological counseling. He paid an out-of-state guy to design his and his business partner's web site.

Apparently there were disagreements on the design and layout; the site they came to a consensus on (below, in Figure 6.1) is one large picture. (I don't want to identify the site so I am only placing a little snippet of the site. There is some text underneath and above in the picture.)

Figure 6.1

It's a nice clean looking site with a spectacular picture on the first landing page. When I started discussing that he needed to have relevant readable text, RSS feeds, links, video, social media items, and more to increase his rankings, he stated, "Do whatever you want, but don't change the look."

Remember way back in chapter 1 when I explained that Google and other search engines see can't read pictures?   Here is what Google sees of this web site (Figure 6.2):

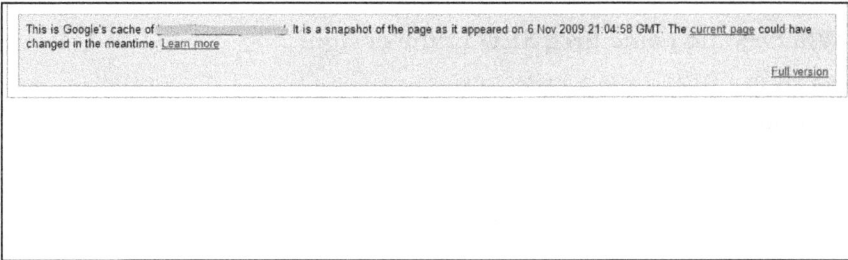

Figure 6.2

That pretty picture on their web site in figure 6.1 is great, isn't it? No it isn't! Why? Because search engines cannot look at the text on pictures and index the information. They can't look at Flash or video either. Now here is the odd part. Having a little of each of those, including relevant text, pictures, video, and Flash, does increase the point ratio that increases your web site's rankings on many of the major search engines.

So, am I going to turn a company that approaches me away for not allowing its web site to be changed to optimize it? No. I am going to consult with them and tell them how to make their web site increase its rankings, which is what I am paid to do. Then I am going to take their money and spend it wisely. I am an expensive person and if someone pays me for advice I am going to give it to them. If they choose not to use my advice, which others find very valuable, I will have no problem taking their money. They got what they paid for.

Also, this is something new that never came up before until this week. If you pay an SEO company to optimize your site during a site redesign, don't change the names of the pages that are indexed with the search engines. When a person does find you and the site file names have been changed, when they click on the link to your site, it won't work. There is a process to doing this if you really want do this later in this chapter.

What should come first, SEO or the design?

This really is the chicken and egg question of the internet marketing age. Depending on who you ask will determine the actual answer you receive.

A graphic designer will argue that in a majority of cases the design comes first, of course. Without an aesthetically pleasing design, a visitor will bounce off your web site within a matter of seconds. But I always say, "Not so fast." How did they get to your web site in the first place? A great-looking web site is nothing if there is no one to look at it.

Even if you intend to employ Google Adwords to advertise your web site, you will soon realize you are spending a fortune to make your sales. That is usually when the SEO expert gets called in because of some research someone did to see how to properly market a web site. Then you learn from your poor design that it will take 6 months or so for the major search engine marketing campaign to try and rescue your web site rankings.

Is this really the best way to go? The thousands of business owners that have been through this exact cycle will certainly argue that it most definitely is not the way you should go, especially when the owners of these sites realized when it was too late the amount of profit, potential, and clients lost because the design looked great to humans but was invisible to the search engines.

What is really laughable, though, is that if you actually read the sales pitch on any one of the myriad of web design companies own web sites, many of them blatantly claim to be SEO experts as if it is a badge of honor or perhaps a must-have tick in the box. However, a quick check of their portfolios soon reveals that if they are search engine marketing experts, then it is clearly evident that their clients are definitely not on the receiving end of any claims they make.

Can you implement site optimization into the design before you launch a web site? Yes! The web design and SEO should go hand in hand. The thought process of optimizing a web site and SEO-friendly web site design should form the foundation right from the outset, so ultimately the content and design will capture free organic search engine traffic and also mark the web site as a potential authority on the product or service.

You should remember that search engines don't care about what the site looks like: it's what's behind the scenes that makes the site so much more relevant to them. However, if we go back to the example above, my new client's initial chance to make the best impact on the search engine when the site first got indexed was wasted. In contrast, the extra time and money spent on predevelopment SEO, including the keyword research and SEO copywriting, gives an outstanding return on the investment of the web site. This also gives you a far better chance of getting good web site ranking from day one and even, in some cases, a page-one result faster than you might think.

If a web designer is not promoting web design SEO as part of your initial client brief, then they are selling you short. Now that you have read this book, even if you have only read Chapter 1, you know how to look at the rankings of their referral sites to see if they know anything about SEO. If your web developers are not SEO experts or if they are not showing results in 6 months in terms of better rankings, the best practice would be to team up with an SEO professional to work with your web designer.

If you are implementing your own SEO, you need to set some SEO design goals for your web site. Let's take a look at the different design or redesign goals for your web site in the next sections to best design your web site for both search engines and visitors.

Goals for Site Design

If your web site is a business, then your web site most likely details the sales aspect of your business. Whether a visitor can buy right there online or has to contact you in other ways the design needs make their experience quick and simple. So when you design your web site, optimizing your web site is one goal, but getting more visitors and leads are another. Only if your web site is easy to use will you meet your goals.

Sidebar: Optimizing For Mobile Devices

Website SEO Professionals has recently started optimizing web sites for mobile web devices. These devices include Blackberries, iPhones, and other mobile web devices that see things in a smaller screen. I haven't even seen this addressed in any books yet. But, as most companies are aware, the mobile Web is becoming more and more important in your web building efforts, which should translate into your SEO efforts as well.

As a company we have been doing Mobile Web SEO for larger enterprise companies for quite a while. As we have researched how to accomplish this, we have collected links on how to make your web site mobile-ready:

- o **Bing Mobile:** discoverbing.com/mobile
- o **Google Mobile:** http://www.google.com/mobile/
- o **Google Mobile Sitemaps:** www.google.com/support/webmasters/bin/answer.py?hl=en&answer=34627
- o **Google Mobile Proxy:** www.google.com/gwt/n
- o **Mobile Search Marketing Guide:** www.mobilesearchmarketing.com/guide.php
- o **Tappity:** www.tappity.com
- o **Technorati Mobile:** http://m.technorati.com
- o **Windows Mobile 2003 Smartphone Emulator:** www.microsoft.com/downloads/details.aspx?familyid=8fe677fa7-3a6a-4265-b8eb-61a628ecd462

Add your mobile-optimized site to search engines and let the world know by placing your web site link on these sites:

- **Abphone:** http://www.abphone.com and http://m.abphone.com
- **Bing:** http:// discoverbing.com/mobile
- **Bango:** http://www.bango.com
- **Crispy:** http://www.crispyweb.com/submitmobile.htm
- **Dotmobi:** http://mtld.mobi/sitesubmit
- Google: http://www.google.com/addurl
- **JumpTap:** http://www.jumptap.com/content-publishers-submit-content
- **Medio:** http://medio.com/partners/addyourmobilesite/
- **Mobiseer**: http://www.mobiseer.com
- **Nokia:** http://europe.nokia.com/A4568518
- **Taptu:** http://taptu.com/a/submit?ps=Q1A9b
- **Sprint:** https://developer.sprint.com/site/global/home/p_home.jsp
- **Vtap:** http://www.vtap.com/index.html

You should focus on the results you want: more visitors, leads, and customers. Every decision you make should be focused on fulfilling those goals. Keeping that in mind, you might spend a bit less time worrying about the exact shade of blue on the callout background, and more time worrying about things that will improve your marketing results and keep visitors directed toward your goals.

There are countless ways a web site design can negatively impact your results. In fact, I would say that more often than not, web site designs done without an SEO professional tend to have a negative impact on marketing results.

Another problem occurs when you attempt to implement too many strategies in your SEO. For one, you won't be able to tell which of your strategies are successful and two, search engines don't like it when you lose focus. Most major search engines like to see each of your web site landing pages centered around one topic.

Implementing one strategy at a time allows you to determine which strategies are working and which strategies are not. SEO campaigns are most successful when you concentrate on one effort at a time.

> **NOTE:** *One of the first things that attracts a search engine's attention is the actual design of your site. The Meta tags, links, navigational structure, and relative content are all focused on a single topic.*

If you have an existing web site you usually have a lot of material that has accumulated over time. These items help your prospects find your web site and help you turn them into leads and customers.

> **WARNING:** *When you do a site redesign, make sure you use the same links and file names for your new site. If you don't, the links that are on search engines will become useless. The proper way to change the site is to create the new pages with new file names. Use the Robot.txt file to tell search engines not to index the old links. In a few months you can get rid of the old files as they will no longer show on the search engines.*

The general rule is, the more content you have the more visitors you will have and the longer they will stay. This will in itself grow your business faster. A 100 page web site will beat a 10 page web site 90% of the time on search engine rankings. And a 500 page web site is even better. if some of those web pages were written recently, that's even better. But remember, always keep the focus of each page as close as you can to a single topic and optimize that page, the Meta Tags, Title, and keyword density to that topic.

A little known rule that helps add to your imaginary point standings with search engine rankings is that the more often you update your content (while keeping it relevant to your web site subject matter), the better.

NOTE: *Blogging makes creating new and updated content easy.*

You want your web site design to attract new visitors and increase your conversion rate and the number of leads you get from your web site. Over time you should constantly improve the effectiveness of your conversion tools, including your landing pages.

If you build a completely static web site and have to go to a web designer, every time you want to set up a new landing page or to change an existing page, you are limiting your ability to quickly experiment and improve on the design. You should have a web site that lets you edit content and build landing pages without having to know web site code unless you know HTML, PHP, or XML well.

One of the rules you should live by is that you should spend money on resources and relevant content that attracts and converts as well as optimizes your site. You should not overdo a design that limits you to only one type of code, such as web sites that include Flash. The code should be dynamic and easy to change. Of course, sometime the easily changed part costs a little more upfront, but not at the end.

If you follow the rules set forth in the last paragraph, you should be able to create ongoing content with a building strategy. When you have more content, you can grow your web site. This will help you increase your visitors and grow your business faster.

When you have finished your web site, you should constantly have conversion experiments. The key to driving your conversion rate and the number of leads you get from your web site over time is to constantly improve the effectiveness of your web site. Several sites can be used to test your web site:

Web site Grader (www.websitegrader.com) – Has a useful tool for measuring the marketing effectiveness of your web site.

AccuQuality (www.AccuQuality.com) – Has the most effective website reporting reports. It have completely accurate reports testing not just the coding but search ability, accessibility, usability, compliance, compatibility with all the browsers, and much more.

Where most only do your home page, AccuQuality reports are much more detailed and cover every page of your website. The errors and recommendations are all backed up by links to describe the issue, how to fix the issue, and it places them in a most critical to least critical fixing order. In my opinion it is the best website report available and I give my personal recommendation.

The Basics in Our Design

We have already hit on the points here, but they fall into this chapter as well. So let's make sure our design or redesign has these points covered:

- Meta and HTML Tags
- Header Tag Content
- Body Text
- Links
- Alternative Tags
- Header Tag Content
- Other Items You Should Make Space For
- Other Valuable Content
- Other Tips

Meta and HTML Tags

Meta tags are HTML tags; they just appear in very specific places on a web page. There are two Meta tags which are given more weight than the others on most search engines. Those are the keyword tag and the description tag.

Most of the Meta tags are also given some weight on less major search engines and directories. However, not all search engines take keyword and description Meta tags into consideration because in the past, these tags have been overloaded with keywords that were irrelevant to the web site.

Header Tag Content

This is a simple attribute but about as commonly overlooked by web designers as the Meta tags are. The *header tags* are a bit different from other tags discussed earlier in this book. These are the attributes that set up the different levels of headings and subheadings on your web site. There can be as many as six different levels of headings but typically search engines only look at the first four.

To help you understand this, the title or topic of a web page should be the H1 title that the human side can see. Subheading of the topic should be tagged with the H2 tag and so on–kind of like a tree (as shown in figure 6.3).

Figure 6.3

So let's say you have a web site that sells fire and safety products. The heading hierarchy in this example should look like this:

    H1: (Page Topic) Fire And Safety Products
    H2: (Main Topic) Fire Products
    H3: (Sub Topic) Hoses
    H3: (Sub Topic) Fire Cabinets
    ...and so on.

If there is a new sub topic such as there is in the example, you would start again with an H2 tag.

    H2: (Main Topic) Safety Products

Headings denote important information and enable users to quickly skim the page to find the information they're seeking. The search engines use this in their scanning of web pages to determine what's vitally important.

Header tags on a web page should contain your most important keywords in a contextually appropriate manner. Specifically, search engine spiders, bots, and crawlers take into consideration the text within a header tags.

Looking at the different levels of headings, first-level headings should contain the most important keywords on your web page.

> **NOTE:** *You should use your most important trophy keywords in the level-one heading, then lower-level headings (levels two through six) should contain decreasingly important keywords.*

The heading tags are similar in format to other tags that you've examined to this point and used after the <Body> tag of the web site:

```
<H1>Header 1</H1>
<H2>Header 2</H2>
<H3>Header 3</H3>
<H4>Header 4</H4>
<H5>Header 5</H5>
<H6>Header 6</H6>
```

> **WARNING:** *Search engines are smart enough to know when your keywords are the same shade or color as your back ground and will penalize you for hiding the H1 tags or text that contains your keywords.*

Header tags should be included before the body-text tags of your web site, and the text of the header goes in between the opening and closing tags.

Body Text

Like the Header tags, the *Body text* is also text that is visible to human readers of your site. When you look at the pages of this book, for example, the text that's between each of the headings would be the body text – the same way as it is for a web page.

The body text is another place where you want to include your keywords. A good rule of thumb is to use your keywords once in every paragraph as long as it makes sense to a reader.

Sidebar: Keywords in Text

Having your keyword strategically placed in your text on every page is one of the most important elements of any web site. Of particular importance are the trophy keywords which we determined in Chapter 2. The trophy keywords need to be placed throughout the text on your primary landing page. It is of particular importance where those keywords appear and how often they appear on the page.

The keywords you choose must match the words and phrases that potential visitors will use when searching for the products or services your web site provides.

You can also use additional tags to indicate special formatting in text. Those tags are as follows:

```
<b>Bold</b>
<i>Italics</i>
<strong>Strongly Emphasized</strong>
<em>Emphasis</em>
<li>New Line in List</li>
```

Each of these special tags indicates special formatting for the word or phrase in between the opening and closing tags, and the special emphasis makes a search engine crawler take notice of those words.

NOTE: *You should try to use keywords within the special tags if possible. Only use keywords where appropriate, and avoid stuffing keywords into your site simply to improve your search engine rankings. If you use those tactics, they will most likely fail and may even get your site banned from some of the search engines.*

Sidebar: Things to Avoid

To make your web site's body text visible to spiders, bots, and crawlers, avoid the following:

- Text embedded in JavaScript applications or Macromedia Flash files cannot been read.
- Text contained in images such as those with extensions .jpg, .gif, .png, and .bmp cannot be seen.
- Text that is accessible only on a submission form is not readable.

Most of these things make your site look flashy and cool. Site designers struggle with these issues and sometime choose looks over site optimization on purpose to make the site owner happy. There are only about 8 different fonts that can be used on a web site without pictures because of the browser standards. Also, certain text styles cannot be indexed by search engines.

If search engine spiders, bots, and crawlers can't see your web site text, then they can't index that content for visitors to find.

Links

You should have an area of your landing page dedicated to links. The links should be related to the content of the page and be active links to real web sites. *Broken links* will lower your search engine rankings on major search engines.

Links have always been an important factor in how web sites rank on the different major search engines. Most important are not only links from your site but to your site as well, as we discussed in Chapter 5.

Alternative Tags

Alternative tags for pictures and links are also important to have on your pages. These are the tags that are a brief description of a picture or graphic on a web site to explain to spiders, bots, and crawlers what is displayed.

These Alt tags are also a good place to include additional keywords to make your site more relevant. Human users will never see your Alt tags unless they intentionally turn off images to enable web pages to load faster.

Other Items You Should Make Space For

Your web site should have some of the below on its main landing pages. The more of these the better. Each one of these increases your site's value on different major search engines.

- A little flash
- Conversion page (submission page)
- RSS Feed
- Video (YouTube if possible. It is owned by Google.)
- Blog (BlogSpot if possible. It is operated by Google.)
- Facebook, MySpace, or Twitter Feed or Widget
- Links to other pages in your body text

- Text links to other pages in your web site if you use pictures, maps, or Flash for buttons.
- Text that can change frequently.

Other Valuable Content

Other Items that can be considered great content:

- A free whitepaper
- A how-to or manual
- A series of articles
- A YouTube video
- A podcast
- A badge or image
- A proprietary study
- A quiz, poll, or test
- A joke or cartoon
- A calculator or free software
- A blog or forum
- A wiki or knowledge base

Other Considerations for Your Web site

For a web site to rank well, the search engines must retrieve information from the web site – not so much from the human side but from the coding side. The retrieval of data is a combination of the activity of the crawler, spider, or bots, the database, and the search algorithm used by each search engine. These three elements work together to retrieve web pages that are related to the word or phrase that a user enters into the search engine's user interface.

The algorithms change frequently, which is one reason this book is updated every year. In SEO, ranking is what you'll spend the most time and effort trying to change. Your ranking in a search engine determines how often people see your page.

How search engines rank a page or pages is a difficult science to figure out and changes frequently. Search engines don't want everyone to know the exact science. If it were known to everyone it would be tough to get on the first or second page of a search.

Ranking is such a large part in search engine optimization and appears frequently throughout book. There are some things that can give your web site an advantage right from the beginning. Let's take a look at two: hosting location and frequency of keyword use.

Hosting Location

There are a lot of locations that we talk about in this book. In this section of the book, I will specifically refer to the location where you host your web site. I have a customer who is in good straights now but had tried to handle his own optimization. No matter what he did he couldn't get his web site off of page 68 on a Google search. At Website SEO Professionals, we do a complete SEO Report to find issues with the web site. What we found was that the web site was being hosted on the same server as several porn-related web sites. In SEO terms we call this being in a "Bad Neighborhood." That is where porn or blacklisted web sites are using the same IP or IP Range as your web site.

In this case, the web site owner had bought his hosting on eBay for $42.00 per year. If you have a respectable business web site, you have to be hosted on a respectable hosting provider. The Major search engines do not like to rank web sites that contain material related to pornography, hate, race, or other such content. Also new to 2011, SEO company related web sites now have to do almost double the work as other industry web sites to maintain the same rankings.

Frequency of Keyword Use

Web sites must be relevant to the keywords you choose. So the frequency with which the keywords appear on a web page may also affect how a page is ranked in search results for that keyword. For example, on a page about office furniture, one that uses the words "office furniture" five times might be ranked higher than one that uses the words only two or three times. When word frequency became a well-known factor, some web site designers began using hidden words hundreds of times on pages, trying to artificially boost their rankings. Almost every search engine recognizes this as *keyword spamming* and ignore or even blacklist pages that use this technique.

Tips

- Don't repeat keywords in your title tags. Repetition can occasionally come across as spam when a crawler is examining your site, so avoid that in your title if possible, and never duplicate words just to gain a spider, bot, or crawler's attention.
- Include a call to action in your title. There's an adage that goes something like, "You'll never sell a thing if you don't ask for the sale." That's true on the Web as well. If you want your users to do something, you have to ask them. The title is never a bad place to ask. But include your trophy keywords there, too.
- Create a web site that contains Meta tags, content, graphics, and keywords that help improve your site ranking.
- Use keywords liberally on your site, so long as they are used in the correct context of your site topic and content. Keep them relevant and search engines will keep you relevant.
- Include reciprocal links to your site from others as long as those links are legitimate and relevant to the topic of your web site.
- Continuously encourage web site traffic through many venues, including keyword advertising, reciprocal links, and marketing campaigns.
- Submit your web site to search engines manually, rather than wait for them to pick up your site in the natural course of cataloging web sites.

Keyword Density

One of the biggest design rules to keep is the number of times you use your keywords (known as *keyword density*). Most search engines allow a relatively low keyword density. Google is by far one of the more lenient in this regard when ranking web sites. Google likes to see a keyword density of 5 to 7 percent – much lower or higher than that and your site is penalized. Bing, Yahoo!, MSN, and other search engines seem to be stricter and want keyword densities of about 6 percent.

Use a Word processing program to find out your total word count. Paste the HTML source code of the page into a blank document, then choose File, Properties, Statistics, Word Count. In Microsoft Office 2007/2010 it is found at File, Prepare, Properties, Statistics.

Let's move on. If you are optimizing that page for a single keyword, you need to figure out how many times that particular word is repeated within that 250 word total.

Manually scan the page and count every repetition of your keyword. If you have Microsoft Word 2007/2010, you should also have an Replace function under the Home tab all the way to the right. Paste in the code and then type in the keywords in both the edit box and the replace box. The program will replace each occurrence of the word with itself...and produce a total count for the number of repeats.

Let's assume for this exercise that you have used a keyword 10 times on your page. To calculate the keyword density - take that figure and divide it by the total number of words on your page. So in this case 10 divided by 250 = .04

Keyword density is always referred to as a percentage of the total word count for the page. So now you need to multiply .04 by 100 to get the percentage figure.

Your calculation would look like this;

.04 x 100 = 4%

The page has a keyword density of 4%.

For effective optimizing that will boost your pages into the Top 20 spots on the major search engines you are aiming for a keyword density of between 5-7%.

What you have just been shown is about as simple as it gets for working out the keyword density of a web page. To recap, the formula looks like this:

10 divided by 250 = .04 x 100 = 4% -or- keyword count divided by total word count x 100 = keyword density in percent. So you can add your keyword another few times without penalty on most major search engines.

Algorithms fluctuate constantly at the major search engines so it is much simpler to optimize a few pages for different weighting or densities. A few pages at 5%, 6%, and 7% keyword density will mean at least one of your pages should rank well on each major search engine.

Chapter 7- Major Search Engines Optimization Differences

Optimization for Major Search Engines
- Optimization for Google
- Optimization for Bing, Yahoo!, MSN, and Microsoft Live

In general, search engine optimization basics are all the same. Each major search engine differs slightly in what it's looking for, however, so what makes you rank well with Google does not make you rank well with Bing (which, incidentally, provides the search results for MSN, Microsoft Live, and now Yahoo!).

It's still up in the air what will happen with smaller search engines that chose Yahoo! to do their search results but it looks like most will be allowing Yahoo! to forward Bing's results. These include:

- AllTheWeb
- AltaVista
- Go
- HotBot
- Lycos

So Bing is really a challenge to Google now.

In the next two sections, we will tell you how to optimize your web site for better rankings with Google. Then we will explain how to optimize your web site for better rankings with Bing. Included is a special report by Jason McCormick with WebSEOPros.com. He has done a three month study testing every aspect of Bing's search results using test web sites which we have optimized and engineered specifically for testing search engine algorithms.

We will also include technical and content suggestions to help you rank higher with both Google and Bing.

Optimization for Google

This book has been focused heavily on Google, as it still maintains the lead in search engine searches. They have lost a lot of ground because of Bing and the millions they poured into an advertising campaign, but are still well above the fifty percent mark in internet searches.

Knowing this, how do you get Google to take notice of your web site? What weights make your site rank higher? We are going to answer this question in this sections.

Google is traditionally, from my experience, the slowest of the major search engines to rank a web site – especially if you have a new domain name. Even if you manually register your site with Google using the steps earlier in the book, it may take months before you can actually type in your domain name and see a result. That doesn't mean it is ranked either. Even with expert SEO it has taken me up to 8 months to get a ranking on a site.

How can you avoid buying a new domain if you are a new business and need a domain name? My recommendation is to buy a domain name from GoDaddy Auctions(www.GoDaddy.com). Every domain you buy from the GoDaddy Auction is at least a year old and some have already had some pretty good SEO work done and there is already links to the domain. Domains are also available on just about any subject or industry.

Google doesn't sell placement, either. There are ads above and to the right side of the search results, but sponsored ads are the only placement that's available for purchase. That means that where your site places is based on your SEO and search engine marketing efforts.

Another heavy weight that adds votes to your web site is the traffic to your web site. You need to install the Google Analytics on your site to enjoy these additional votes to help improve the rankings on your web site.

> **NOTE:** *Recently a lot of weight has been added to the Title Tag if it matches the first three keywords in the Meta Tags, the description contains the first three words, and the keyword density is around 7%.*

Google PageRank

Google has a proprietary ranking algorithm and although they trademarked some parts of it, it changes frequently. An element of that algorithm is called Google PageRank.

Google explains PageRank like this:

> *"PageRank relies on the uniquely democratic nature of the Web by using its vast link structure as an indicator of an individual page's value. In essence, Google interprets a link from page A to page B as a vote, by page A, for page B. But, Google looks at considerably more than the sheer volume of votes, or links a page receives; for example, it also analyzes the page that casts the vote. Votes cast by pages that are themselves "important" weigh more heavily and help to make other pages "important." Using these and other factors, Google provides its views on pages' relative importance.*

Google PageRank is based on a balloting system that compares your site to all the other pages on the web that are of the same topic or topics. Then their algorithms take all the indexed information on those sites to determine which pages are most relevant to a search query based on numerous elements of the page.

An inbound link to a page counts as a vote of support, so links as discussed in Chapter 9 are very important. A page that is linked to by many pages with high PageRank receives a high rank if all the other components of optimization are in place. If there are no links to a web page, there is no support for that page. You will rarely find a page ranked by Google without inbound links. Know what the keyword density is or how well the other components of optimization are performed.

Google Webmaster Tools

Google has some general guidelines if you want to rank successfully. These guidelines and recommendations are laid out on Google's Webmaster Central (www.google.com/webmasters) which we explained in Chapter 4. You will also find tools available at Webmaster Central that enable you to analyze your site to help make it more Google-friendly. Those tools include the following:

- **Site Status Wizard**: This tool helps you to determine whether your site is currently being indexed by Google.
- **Webmaster Tools:** A set of tools designed to help you improve the indexing and ranking of your site.

146

- **Google Site Map Generator:** Under the Webmaster Tools you can find the Google Sitemap Generator to make a sitemap of your web site.

- **Content Submission Tools:** This tools is used to submit your site to Google, or to add products to Google Base or content to Google Book Search.

- **Google's Webmaster Blog:** Here you can find tips and strategies for ranking well in Google. Also you will find information on how the Google algorithm has changed.

- Webmaster Help Center: If you don't understand something about Webmaster Central, here's where you'll find an explanation.

Google Instant

Google added "Google Instant" in September of 2010 which showed a new feature of the Google interface designed with a new search engine algorithm to improve the user experience. Google Instant is really about showing you more search results and keeping you from going to page 2 of a search.

The way it works is simple, Google Instant turns a search into a real-time stream of results which flow onto your screen as you type your query as shown below in Figure 7.1 as I start typing in a search for electric cars.

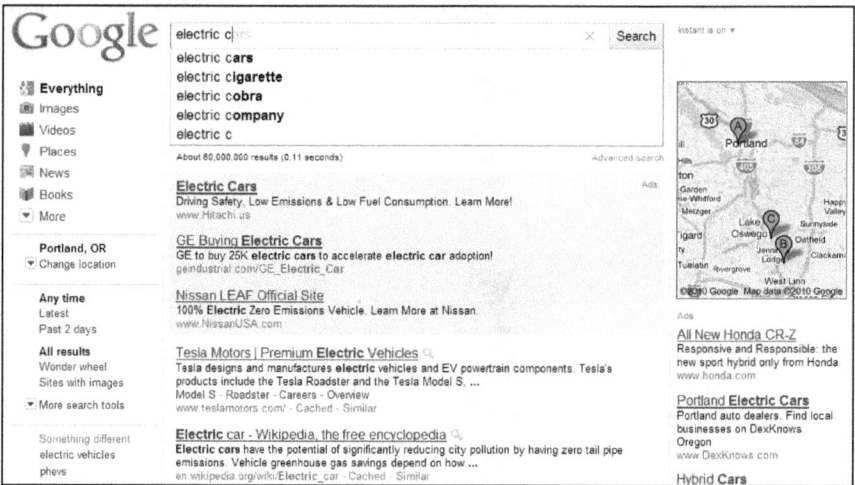

Figure 7.1

With each letter you type, a whole new set of results displays on the screen. This is important for several reasons. First, you will now see many more search results than you would have otherwise. Most people never click through to the second page of search results so this is a way for Google to display several more pages of results.

If it is not in the first ten blue links (or really the first five or six), it might as well not exist for most people. With a Google Instant search, instead of people seeing only ten results, they may now see 50 or 100 (depending on how many letters they type and how far they get through each search query).

After testing the changes brought on by testing the results of Google Instant, several configurations clearly have an advantage. Those websites who have the key search words in their domain name or as the very first word(s) in the title that the users are searching for are not really effected by the change. Also those websites who have changed their pages to be completely relevant for only one keyword or one long-tail keyword are reaping the rewards of Google Instant.

From here on out you need to look at your pages and either modify your current pages or add pages so that your pages are optimized for only a single search terms or the search term and the plural version. As an example, if your website sells golf balls you would focus on the plural first and the singular second now in case they complete the whole keyword as shown below:

Golf Balls | Golf Balls

Don't focus your page on more than one keyword now. You should also have the keywords in your Meta Keywords tag and in the Meta Description tag as well. If you don't know what I am talking about, refer back to Chapter 2.

For many large websites creating new pages focusing on just one product, service, or keyword is a burden, but the sooner the changes are made, the sooner you will reap the rewards. Many companies are seeing their full keyword position not changing with the full keyword and do not realize they are losing visits because they are not optimized for Google Instant.

According to Google, its classic search interface took nine seconds on average for each search results to be returned. The new interface utilizing Google Instant algorithm shaves off about 2-5 seconds per search.

iGoogle

Other useful tools for improving your search engine rankings are the various Google APIs (Application Programming Interfaces) that are available at iGoogle.com, as shown in figure 6.4. These programming interfaces enable you to use Google technology to do many things, but most are geared toward improving the optimization of your web site.

Figure 6.4

There are many help tools on the site to help you optimize your web site. Many of them are pay-to-use tools, but usually you can find a free tool to do the same thing as the paid ones.

The use of Google APIs should be limited to creating applications and gadgets that your site visitors find useful. When you fulfill a need, visitors to your site continuously return, and that builds momentum. This in turn improves your search rankings simply on the merits of traffic and usability. That's a great vote for your site and Google will notice.

Google Instant Preview

You might have noticed, the Google Search Engine Results Pages (SERPs) have changed. Upon first glance, it still has a familiar feel, but everything is different. Google Instant Previews which can be found at http://www.google.com/landing/instantpreviews, is a visual preview or pop-up of a website in the results before you click through to the website.

It also looks as though Previews is improving click-through rates directly from the SERP. Recent testing by Google shows Previews makes searchers 5-10 percent more likely to be satisfied with the results they click.

150

Five percent improvement is significant enough to expect more changes in the future as well. There is a strong possibility that query results will begin to be served in large part from the outcome of the selections made from Google Instant Previews. Serving intent-targeted results could become a defining factor for search engine rankings.

The preview of the website is now shown in the SERP and then the mouse hovering over the page creates a click-through which can be used as a ratio. This could be serving results based more on the user's evaluations of the website image and content from the SERP. The users see what they like and they click through as shown in Figure 6.5 where my website is displayed in the preview.

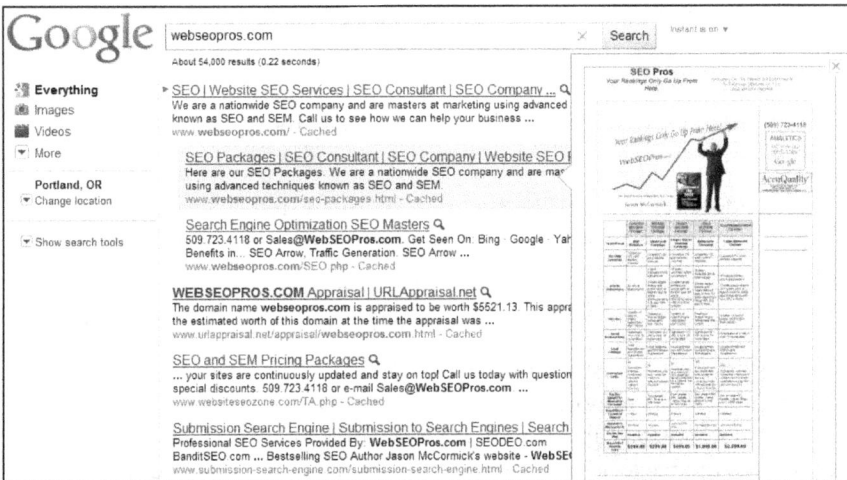

Figure 6.5

Google Instant Previews has been proven to increase click-through rates and drive conversion and we will see a push to serve more results based on previews. There will be new criteria to take into consideration for SEO as conversion and a better user viewing experience. Below is our instructions on doing just that:

- Keep your pages clearly laid out and structured, with a minimum of distractions or extraneous content especially in the top fold of your websites homepage or landing pages.

- Utilizing larger fonts that can be read in a small screen.

- Keep the upper fold of your homepage or landing pages simple and clear of your site will be apparent via Instant Previews.

- Try to avoid interstitial pages, ad pop-ups, or other elements that will interfere with your content being seen in a small screen.

- Make your pages enticing using compelling graphics that are relevant to the keyword they are using to search for your product or service. (If you have distracting or small content it will be picked up in the preview of your page, making the screenshot the searcher sees less attractive.)

- My personal recommendation is to start making your website look like a billboard in the upper fold.

Why would Google do this? The answer is simple, more accurate search results. By allowing the user to decide the relevancy of a Web page before a click-through, the results served will be more accurate by default. So your pages must be enticing from the get-go.

The next reason is "More Money". By Google serving the most accurate results faster and easier, people will use Google more, which will in turn drive revenue.

- Spam reduction: The accuracy of the results will likely make it more difficult for spammers to artificially influence search results.

- Sales conversions: By improving conversions on the Internet across the board, Google will increase revenue by default.

When trying to understand the reasons behind Google's changes to the search engines, it's important to remember why any company does what they do. The bottom line: To improve the products and make more money. In the back of your mind however, you have to remember Google is an Internet veteran that does not usually make changes that aren't related to bettering its financial position..

As SEO analysts, we are much more like detectives in a crime scene. We analyze and decipher what our customer need to do to stay on top.

By the way. To keep your website from being shown in Google Instant Previews (Which is probably a bad idea.) all you have to do is enter this line in your Meta tagging:

```
<meta name="googlebot" content="nosnippet">
```

Google Caffeine

Google Caffeine is a quicker way to index websites to improve how fast Google can deliver relevant new content. The main change is Google is indexing less of each page and putting more relevancy on the "above the fold" area of the viewable content on each website page. (The top of the website page.)

My recommendations to you is to make your website 100% relevant in the 800x600 viewable area at the top of each webpage for your keywords and stop hiding content at the bottom of your web pages. Use a perfect keyword density, a relevant <H1> tag, all the links to your social media, and limit the pictures at the top of your web pages for the best results.

Google Surveys

Google surveys are a great way to let Google and your target audience know that you are important. You will need two items in place before you can begin creating a Google Survey for your homepage; a Google account that you can log into to use Google Docs and a clear idea of the question you want to ask and some possible answers to your question from which your visitors can choose.

1. Log in to your Google account and click the "Documents" link in the drop down menu under the "more" link at the top of the Google homepage.
2. Click on the "Create new" drop down menu directly under the "Google docs" in the upper left corner and choose "form". This opens the Edit Form application.
3. Type a title for your survey in the field marked "Untitled form".
4. Beneath the title field is a larger box marked "You can include any text or info that will help people fill this out". You may wish to add an explanation of your survey. This is optional.
5. Type your question in the **Question Title** field marked "Sample Question 1".
6. Skip the **Help Text** field and choose "Multiple choice" from the **Question Type** drop down menu.
7. Type possible answers to your survey question within each radio button field. This could be as simple as "yes" or "no", or have a number of longer answers such as "I feel strongly about the question", "I am indifferent to the question", etc.
8. Below the answer fields click on the checkbox labeled **Make this a required question**. This will insure that your visitor must answer the question before they can submit the form.
9. Click "DONE".
10. If you want add a "Sample Question 2" or even more questions. However, keep in mind that many people will not wish to take your survey if it looks too long and complicated.
11. You may also wish to select a Theme from the templates that Google offers that matches your homepage background or in some way seems to fit your website's design. Do this by clicking on the "Theme" button in the top menu of the form application.

12. Click the "Save" button in the top menu. You may also wish to see what your survey looks like now by clicking on the "view the published form" link at the bottom of the form application.

13. You can go back and edit your form. To edit the questions click on the little pencil icon to the right of your question. Remember to "Save" after any editing.

14. You can now ready to publish your survey to your homepage (or blog). Click the "More actions" button in the top menu and choose "Embed". A pop-up box will display the code you can cut and paste into an appropriate spot on your website. It will look like this:

```
<iframe
src="http://spreadsheets.google.com/embeddedform?formkey=dGJFTGtPbDcyQ2
syODhMLTgwQ3pUd0E6MQ" width="760" height="722" frameborder="0"
marginheight="0" marginwidth="0">Loading...</iframe>
```

15. You can later view the responses to your survey by logging into Google Docs and clicking on the form in your list of documents (it will have a small green checkmark icon). This will bring up a spreadsheet with a date stamp and answer for each response. You can also view a graphical summery of your survey by clicking on "View summary of responses" from the drop down Form menu at the top of the spreadsheet.

Google Technical Suggestions:

- ✓ Make sure your domain name is registered for at least a year or more.
- ✓ Install Google Analytics to measure traffic to increase rankings.
- ✓ Match the first three keywords on the Title tag, Meta descriptions tag, Meta keyword tag.
- ✓ Focus on only 1-3 keywords on a page.
- ✓ Keep the keyword density for the first word around 7%, 6% for the second word, and 4% for the third.
- ✓ Validate your HTML code.
- ✓ Avoid broken links.
- ✓ Ensure that you have allowed the GoogleBot to crawl your site and employ Robots.txt.
- ✓ Use static URLs wherever possible rather than dynamic URLs with multiple extensions.
- ✓ Interact with Google owned sites such as Blogger, BlogSpot, and YouTube.

Google Content Suggestions:

- ✓ Don't use a newly registered domain name.
- ✓ Create valuable content.
- ✓ With visible on-page text, include keywords.
- ✓ Keep pages down to a reasonable file size.
- ✓ Try not to cover more than one topic per page.
- ✓ Use static text links.
- ✓ Put keywords in text rather than in images.

Optimization for Bing, Yahoo!, MSN, & Microsoft Live

MSN and Microsoft Live are powered by Bing. In a short time Bing has become one of the top three search engines, and it's definitely not one that you should ignored – especially since Yahoo! partnered with Bing to produce Yahoo!'s search results and do advertising. This is making Yahoo! and Bing serious competition for Google.

This is one section that gives you a reason to throw last year's SEO books away for sure! As with other search engines, the basic optimization techniques that you've learned are the best way to get your site listed in Bing's database. Bing does not allow paid rankings, so your organic efforts will be the deciding factor for your rankings.

The one difference with Bing is that this search engine puts more emphasis on the freshness of content than other search engines. Specifically, sites that update high-quality, relevant content on a regular basis have a better chance of ranking high with Bing. Therefore, if you have not yet implemented a content renewal strategy and you want to rank well with Bing, you should plan and implement a strategy as quickly as you can.

Figuring out Bing's algorithm has been a task that two of our best SEO technicians here are Website SEO Professionals have been solely devoted to. More emphasis was given to this project when Bing announced it would take over search and advertising for Yahoo!

Bing Algorithm Summary of Overall Findings

Over the past three months I have done experiments with our test web sites to figure out the key weights that Bing uses to decide rankings and return results from user searches. I have determined the following factors weigh more heavily in Bing's algorithms:

- Location Meta Tags in Long-tail Searches.
- Content and keyword density of around 6%.
- Excellent and continuously renewing content.
- Rich content (even more important on Bing than just about anything else).
- Keyword placement. Making sure you have your keywords in all the right places is imperative with the Bing search engine,

especially page titles, H1 tags, and link text. They must all use matching trophy keywords.

- Authoritative inbound links. News organizations are especially ranked higher for inbound links. Inbound links are important for any major search engine, but Bing appears to act even more favorably toward inbound links, particularly those that are from sites that are news-oriented and have a high number of links.
- A technically sound, well-built site. Validating your code is important. You are penalized heavily for broken links.
- An XML Sitemap is absolutely required, as is a link to it placed under the web site's listing in the Bing Webmaster Center.

Bing offers quite a few Web sites and tools to help site owners ensure their sites are well positioned for indexing within the engine. Bing Webmaster Center, which we explained in Chapter 4, provides lots of helpful documentation and tools, including technical and content guidelines similar to Google's Webmaster Tools.

There's also a Webmaster blog, which contains a useful section on search marketing. As part of the Webmaster Center, Bing offers "Guidelines to Successful Indexing" to help Web site owners ensure that the MSNBot can index all of your web site's content.

Bing Technical Suggestions:

- ✓ Validate your HTML code.
- ✓ Avoid broken links.
- ✓ Set up redirects from old pages to new ones.
- ✓ Ensure that you have allowed the MSNBot to crawl your site and employ Robots.txt.
- ✓ Keep the keyword density around 6%.
- ✓ Use static URLs wherever possible rather than dynamic URLs with multiple extensions.

Bing Content Suggestions:

- ✓ Create valuable content.
- ✓ With visible on-page text, include keywords.
- ✓ Keep pages down to a reasonable file size.
- ✓ Try not to cover more than one topic per page.
- ✓ Use static text links.
- ✓ Put keywords in text rather than in images.

Chapter 8-Pay-Per-Click (PPC)

This chapter will focus on the top two Pay-Per-Click companies Google and Bing. Why? Because there were three – Google AdWords, Yahoo! Search Marketing, and Microsoft AdCenter. Now however, Bing which is owned by Microsoft and is now doing advertising for Yahoo!

There are others, including MySpace and Facebook, but these are the two with the greatest reach for your money. Between the two they represent both a majority of the directories and search engines on the internet.

Pay-per-click marketing is an advertising method that enables you to buy search engine placement by bidding on keywords or phrases. When people search using your chosen keywords, and you have bid an amount that will place you on a page a user is looking at, your ad will appear in the sponsored listings to the right or above the organically-placed web sites, regardless of how your site ranks on any search engine.

Now before we start, PPC management is an exact science and I don't recommend that you do this yourself. There is a reason why there are companies such as mine that do PPC management for a fee.

If you aren't organically at the top of the search engines and you are a business that relies on your web site for business, then you have to use PPC to draw in visitors to your web site. PPC ads are paid ads which show up at the top or the sides of search engine listings and are sometimes called "Sponsored Listings." They also are placed on web sites and other search engines associated with the search engine you are doing your marketing on.

Should I continue PPC after I have good organic placement?

The answer is yes! There are many reasons. Number one is you cannot guarantee that your organic placement will stay at the top. There are always other competing companies who will inevitably do their own SEO work to get ahead of your company. Sometimes a competitor will wind up in the news and all those news stories will show up before your company's listing. You could wind up on the second or third page for a month or two. Not only that, sometimes you drop down the organic list for no apparent reason at all.

This can really hurt sales and is sometimes not noticeable right away, unless you are checking Google and Bing every day for your keywords. However, if you are always running a PPC campaign to supplement your organic listings, you'll see your company name more than once on the screen. It also guarantees that no matter what happens with your organic placement, the keywords used on your PPC campaign will always be there.

If you are looking for a company to do your PPC campaign, there are some qualifying questions you should ask:

- How long has this company been around? You don't want a company that is new to the industry. Find out how much experience the owners have.
- What features and feature combinations does the company provide? Are there packages that include SEO, SEM, as well as PPC? Your company requirements might differ from other companies. Look at the different features and feature combinations that are offered.
- Do they have all inclusive packages or is this a service that has no fixed costs? If they don't have a fixed cost, you may be getting a bill for far more than you could ever imagine.
- How many campaigns can you run simultaneously? Some PPC management companies restrict the number of PPC campaigns you can run at any one time. Others have restrictions on the types of campaigns you can run as they only do local campaigns and not national or international ones.
- Does the company have client referrals? Client referrals are an often overlooked aspect of PPC company research. There should be a plethora of clients that are satisfied by the company. I know that with WebSEOPros.com I have a list of 20 clients or so I like to give as referrals. Each one will tell you that our services are unbelievable.

Some companies have dozens or even hundreds of pay-per-click campaigns running at any given time. Keeping up with all those ads and campaigns can be a real challenge; if it's not your core capability, it could take you away from activities that would be more profitable for your company.

In fact, I have two companies I manage which have two project managers to keep track of the campaigns. There are daily tasks that require companies to hire PPC management firms to take care of the daily tasks involved in running all those PPC campaigns.

It's not as easy as signing on to Google and giving them your credit card. You can do that but you will be wasting thousands of dollars for very little results. Just like SEO, PPC is almost an exact science and it changes frequently as well.

For instance, there is keyword research, writing ad copies, tracking analytics, determining the return on investment (ROI) for each campaign, and any of the other tasks that attend pay-per-click campaigns.

Return on Investment (ROI) Formula

Return on investment (ROI) is a term that you'll hear frequently throughout this chapter. It is associated with keyword advertising. PPC advertising is becoming increasingly expensive – you need a way to justify your keyword investments with solid returns and a way to measure the PPC campaign's effectiveness.

There are a number of formulas for determining the ROI. For my customers, I use a straight forward formula:

ROI = [Contribution] / [Cost]

To calculate Contribution for a PPC campaign:

([Your average profit per sale] x [Estimated number of Conversions]) – [PPC Cost]

To demonstrate, let's take the following example:

Monthly PPC Cost:	$1,500
Average Profit per Sale:	$ 50
Number of Conversions (Sales) per Month:	75

This would make the break down the following:

($50 x 75) – $1500 = $2,250

So your ROI would be:

$2,250 / $1500 = 150%

The services provided by PPC management firms can cost you anywhere from about $500 per month for basic services to as much as a $250,000 flat fee for a complete campaign-management package over a specified amount of time. The question is whether it's worth it for you to pay this fee to free up your time and get the right expertise involved.

For a successful campaign, the answer is most likely "yes." A PPC management firm might be just what you need to help reduce the burden of managing single or multiple PPC campaigns and doing the job right. Just make sure you know what you're getting into before you sign a contract.

Since there is no contract yet, let's look at how to start your own campaign with Google AdWords and the Microsoft AdCenter in the next few sections.

The funny thing about this section is that it went through major changes in 2009 and virtually every new SEO book I picked up, even the ones for 2011 have the old AdWords screens in their books and giving all the wrong information.

Oh, and another thing that people sometimes get confused about. Many people mistakenly believe that PPC and paid-inclusion (PI) services are the same type of marketing, but there are major differences. For starters, paid-inclusion services are used by some search engines to enable web site owners to pay a one-year subscription fee to ensure that their site is indexed with that search engine at all times.

This fee doesn't guarantee any specific rank in search engine results; it only guarantees that the site is indexed by the search engine. PPC costs money when a searching user clicks on a link advertised in the sponsored listings of a page. You pay each time a user clicks on the link to your site or landing page.

Google AdWords

Since Google still has a leading edge over all the other major search engines combined, it makes sense that AdWords is the PPC component you hear the most often. AdWords is a challenge even for the most informed and talented. I cannot tell you how many times an I.T. guru from a company came through our company doors to inquire about having us manage their ad campaigns. They tell of how they have spent thousands on AdWords campaigns and got a lot of clicks but never a sale or very few sales. Why? Because it is again almost an exact science from the keywords you choose, the wording of your ad, bidding for placement, all the way to the landing page that each ad goes to.

Most think they can learn it all from an eBook they bought online or bought at a store. It is very easy to give your credit card to Google and wind up with a $1200.00 bill and not a single phone call if you don't know what you are doing.

One of the biggest stumbling blocks is when you choose too broad of a keyword. I will give you an example. One of my clients owns a private gym here in Tualatin, Oregon. He tried his own PPC campaign and chose every keyword he could think of remotely related to gyms, exercise, and equipment. Less than two weeks later he noticed his credit card had been billed $500 (Google bills the card every time the amount reaches $500) seven times for a total of $3,500 by the time he got his credit card statement, with not one call that he could think of. He had been expecting to spend around $250.00 per month.

You can imagine his frustration and disbelief. It didn't deter him, but he tried some other things and set limits. Month after month he increased those limits until it matched what he was spending on telephone book ads, which did nothing for him anymore. Month after month, no results but lots of clicks. To the tune of $2,000. Which was spent usually within the first 10-14 days of the month.

He sat down with us and we took a look at some of the things he was doing with his PPC campaign. He was using 44 keywords which we reduced down to only 12. Because he had no clue about researching keyword costs he chose keywords that were at a national level and not local, but also had so much competition that he spent up to $25.00 for a single click!

Keep this rule in mind. Placement costs for ads is based on how much competition there is for a keyword. You actually bid on placement for those keywords. If there is a lot of competition you can spend a fortune quick.

His next major problem was that he chose words such as "exercise equipment" and "gym membership." These are great keywords on a national level but you have people all over the nation clicking on his ads and they live in other states or nowhere close to Tualatin, Oregon. So he wasted his money on people clicking on his ads who would never become a customer or even bother to call.

Next issue is that "exercise equipment" is too broad and there is too much competition. Someone searching for "exercise equipment" might be looking to buy exercise equipment, to repair exercise equipment, or to donate exercise equipment. They might be looking for new exercise equipment or used exercise equipment. The list goes on. The point I am trying to make: very few of those clicking were looking to get a gym membership.

Keep in mind that he had 30 more words that had similar or less critical flaws. I didn't mean to make this sound like a sales pitch but the fact is, if you are not expert, don't try to make yourself one overnight.

I now handle all of SEO and PPC campaigns for Mark Romine, the owner of the gym I mentioned above. Mark spent virtually every hour of his workday for an entire two months to try and get his campaign done right and failed. He graciously allowed me to use his name in this book on the condition that I printed this statement:

> *"If you use my name, make sure your readers know that as a business owner, they should spend their time doing other things selling and growing their business. I wasted more than $7,500 trying to do an AdWords [campaign] before one of my customers recommended Jason McCormick at WebSEOPros.com.*
>
> *You guys get the results I wanted and more for about $500.00 per month. I get 500 times the business from my web site then I do from the *** telephone book which I spend $2,100 per month on by the way."*

He went on to state why he still had to keep an ad in the phone book but basically it was because he has a senior demographic which is about the only demographic besides the telephone ad sales people that crack open a telephone book.

Now being the biggest doesn't always mean being the best. When you're evaluating the different PPC companies you might use, be sure to check not only the traffic rate, but also the conversion rate, if possible. It's great if your ads receive a lot of impressions. If those impressions don't turn to clicks, you'll find that your PPC campaign is not at all effective.

> **NOTE:** *An impression is every time someone performs a search on one of your chosen keywords and your ad is displayed on the screen. Google tracks this information as well as the clicks. Also tracked are the numbers of times a particular keyword was clicked on, the ad that was used when it was clicked, and the cost.*
>
> *Another thing to note is that if you have more than one ad for the keywords you use, Google will alternate between them in the beginning. If, however, a particular ad is clicked on more often, Google will automatically show on the more popular ad a greater percentage of the time and will sometimes stop creating impressions of the non-performing ad altogether.*

One thing that many people don't know is that Google also offers TV, newspaper, and embedded-video advertising. Even the radio and phone models of AdWords are charged on a bid-per-keyword basis. To make things even more complicated, AdWords is linked to Google's AdSense program, which is an advertisement publishing program whereby web site owners place ads on their web sites with similar relevancy to your ads – sometimes competing sites. When users click through those ads and make purchases, the web site owner is paid a small amount. Many web site owners use this service to help offset the cost of having a site or to make money.

Just like Bing has many other search engines they provide results for, Google provides the search and advertising results for many other search engines and web sites. So if you place an ad with Google, your ad will show in the results on AOL Search, Ask.com, and Netscape as well.. This helps give Google AdWords to be one of the largest providers available for keyword advertisements.

A larger market, however, does not necessarily mean better results or a guarantee of higher-quality leads. With Google AdWords, it's essential that you pay attention to the details that help place your ads, and learn the science of Internet ad placement so your ads are the most effective for their cost. This requires research.

As an example, when doing research for a fire and safety company that I do the SEO and PPC for, I realized that there was so much competition and the cost was so great on Google that Microsoft's AdCenter made more sense.

The competition for the fire- and safety-related keywords was primarily focused on Google and was quite low on Bing and its related search engines. Although there are less clicks, the ratio of competing web sites to clicks gave my client an advantage. The numbers of competing ads were smaller to. We still use the keywords on Google AdWords but we focused on the more competitive keywords on Microsoft AdCenter and it is really paying off for the client, who now has a 5 to 1 ratio some months – at a much lower cost. Giving the customer a great ROI.

Signing up for Google AdWords

Signing up for Google AdWords is quick and easy. You can get there by going to http://www.google.com/services and choosing the link to AdWords or the "Get Started" button, as shown in figure 8.1.

Advertise your business with Google AdWords

Google AdWords lets you promote your business alongside relevant Google search results and on our advertising network. Reach people looking for information about your products and services online. Easily control your budget and target prospects geographically. Learn more »

Get Started

Maximize revenue from your online content

Google AdSense enables website publishers of all sizes to display relevant ads on their online content and earn money. AdSense supports a wide variety of online media including websites, mobile, video, games and feeds. Learn more »

Increase website conversions and marketing ROI

Use Google Analytics easy-to-understand reports to make measurable improvements to campaigns and websites. Learn which keywords, sites and locations bring high-value traffic, and be more informed about how visitors are reacting to your site's content. Learn more »

All of our business solutions

Reach new customers

AdWords
Advertise your business on Google

Your ads can appear when people search Google or visit our network of partner sites.

Enhance your website

AdSense
Earn revenue from your website

AdSense delivers ads precisely targeted to your site, helping you earn revenue from your website.

Increase your productivity

Google Enterprise Search solutions
Search company information

New! Maximize website ROI and internal productivity with Google-powered search for your website or intranet.

Figure 8.1

If you have a Google account you can enter it and sign it. Otherwise you need to choose "Start Now" and create an account, as shown in figure 8.2.

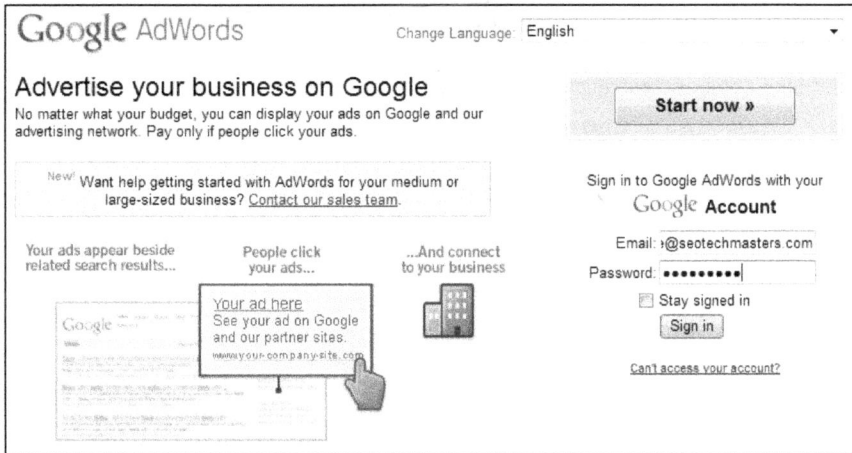

Figure 8.2

If you press "Start Now," you are given the option of using an existing Google account or creating a new account specifically for AdWords. After selecting, login as shown in figure 8.3.

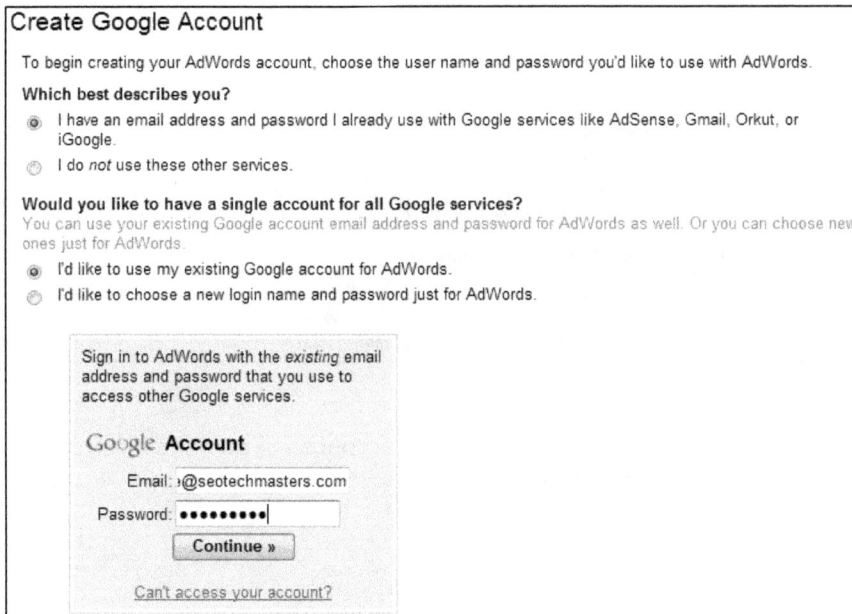

Figure 8.3

Your next screen allows you to set the country, time zone, and the type of currency you use, as shown in figure 8.4. You have to remember that Google is a worldwide search engine and not just a U.S. search engine.

Set time zone and currency preferences

To set up your AdWords account, we need to know your time zone and currency (This is the currency you'll use to pay Google, not the currency you use in transactions with your customers).

Select a permanent time zone for your account.
This will be the time zone for all your account reporting and billing.

Time zone country or territory:	United States ▼
Time zone:	(GMT-08:00) Pacific Time ▼

Select a permanent currency for your account.
Review the available payment options for local currencies before you decide. Not all currencies are available in all areas.

US Dollar (USD $) ▼

Your time zone and currency settings can't be changed after you setup your account.
Please review your choices carefully and then click 'Continue.'

Back | Continue

Figure 8.4

After you press "Continue," your AdWords account is created, as shown in figure 8.5.

Your AdWords account has been created

Next step: Create your first ad campaign.

Login Email: mike@seotechmasters.com

You can now sign in to your AdWords account using the Google Account address and password you just specified. When you sign in, you'll be asked to create your first ad campaign and enter your billing information to activate your account and start running your ads. We'll also send an activation email with more details to the address listed above.

Your ad won't run until you submit your billing information.

Sign in to your AdWords account

Start learning how to make the most of your AdWords account by reading our optimization tips.

Figure 8.5

Press the link "Sign into your AdWords account." You are redirected to login, as shown in figure 8.6.

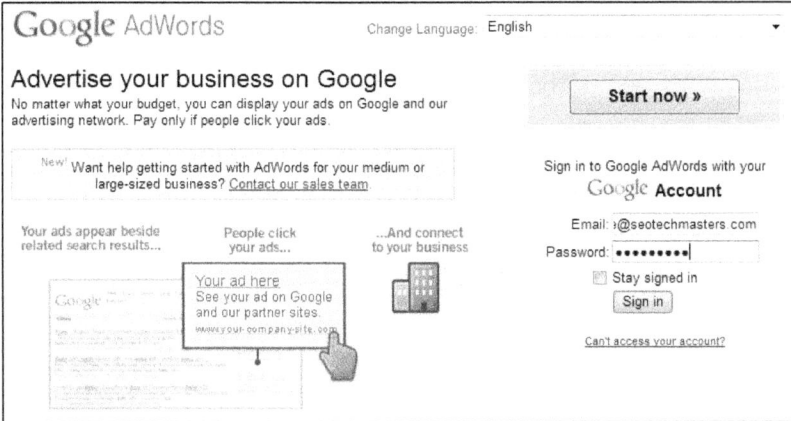

Figure 8.6

When you first login, Google will give you the option to learn more about Google AdWords in figure 8.7. Keep in mind that there is useful information on the link, but in my opinion, it gives you just enough information to be dangerous. The instructions teach you to use the broadest range of keywords for clicks. Well that makes Google the most amount of money.

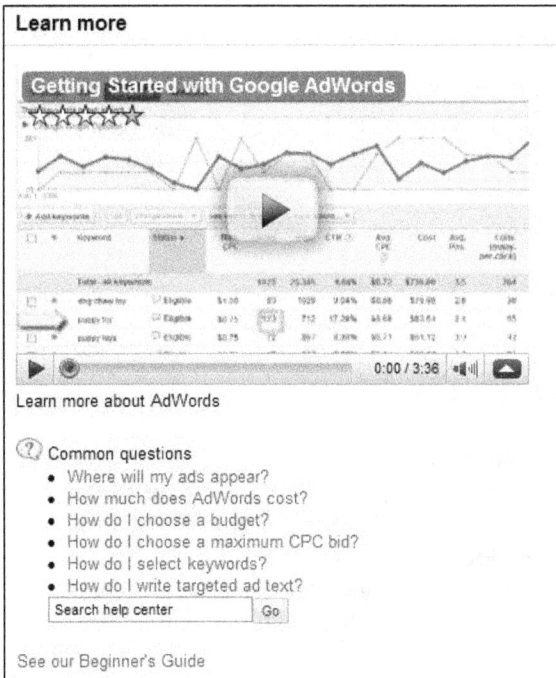

Figure 8.7

If you look to the left of the screen, you have the option to create your first campaign. Click here and begin, as shown in figure 8.8.

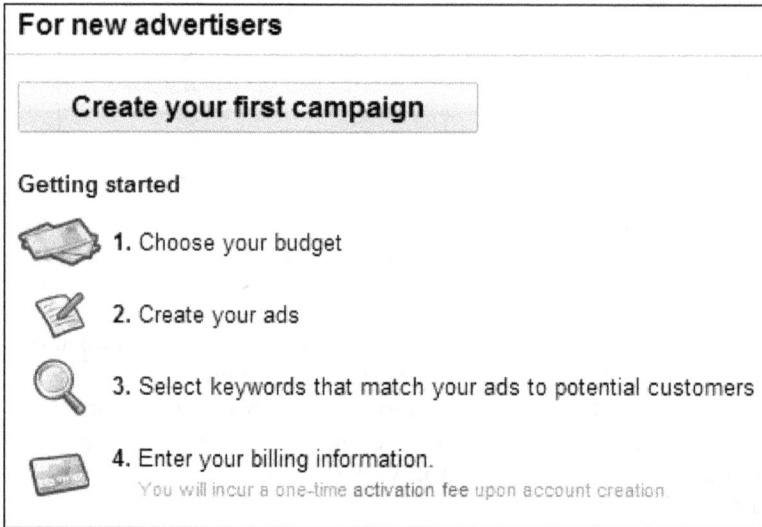

For new advertisers

Create your first campaign

Getting started

1. Choose your budget

2. Create your ads

3. Select keywords that match your ads to potential customers

4. Enter your billing information.
   You will incur a one-time activation fee upon account creation

Figure 8.8

Keep in mind, this is one of Google's primary income sources and there are a lot of stockholders to pay.

Then you begin the registration process, which configures the basic edition of AdWords. The basic edition is great if you've never used a PPC program before. It includes one set of keywords, basic reporting capabilities, and basic targeting.

> **Note:** *At the bottom of the screen of figure 8.8 there is an option to create Advanced Campaigns. This type of campaign is for very experienced users and creates multiple sets of keywords and more advanced targeting and reporting, in addition to a few other tools.*

You can begin with the basic starter edition, then you can graduate to the an advanced campaign when you're ready. When you do, your starter campaign will be moved to your new AdWords account, so you don't lose any of your existing advertisements.

Next, Google wants to know about your business, as shown in figure 8.9. This is to give you advice on the types of ads you should run.

Figure 8.9

The questions in figure 8.9 are primarily for novice users. There is a link to disregard Google's advice and go straight to the campaign. I am going to move on and create a campaign for my awesome, make-believe furniture company called "Orlando Furniture Stuff," as shown in figure 8.10.

Figure 8.10

I can also choose an additional demographic such as ages, locations, occupation and much more by clicking on the "Demographic (advanced)" option.

Next you choose where you would like your ads to be seen, as shown in figure 8.11. This screen can also protect you from click fraud. (We will discuss click fraud in more depth later in this chapter.) If you find yourself the victim of click fraud, you can change your "Network, devices, and extensions" setting based on where the fraud is occurring.

Networks, devices, and extensions

Networks ⑦　　○ All available sites (Recommended for new advertisers)
　　　　　　　⦿ Let me choose...
　　　　　Search　☑ Google search
　　　　　　　　　☑ Search partners (requires Google search)
　　　　　Content　☑ Content network
　　　　　　　　　⦿ Relevant pages across the entire network
　　　　　　　　　○ Relevant pages only on the placements I manage

Devices ⑦　　○ All available devices (Recommended for new advertisers)
　　　　　　　⦿ Let me choose...
　　　　　　　☑ Desktop and laptop computers
　　　　　　　☑ iPhones and other mobile devices with full Internet browsers

Bidding and budget

Bidding option ⑦　Basic options | Advanced options
　　　　　　⦿ Manual bidding for clicks

　　　　　　♀ You'll set your maximum CPC bids in the next step.

　　　　　　○ Automatic bidding to try to maximize clicks for your target budget

Budget ⑦　$ 200.00 per day
　　　　　Daily budget represents your average spend over the month; actual spend on a given day may vary.

Figure 8.11

In figure 8.12, there are some optional advanced settings. For instance, you can choose where you want your ad to show and the delivery method. The defaults are shown.

Next, you can change the dates your ad run, set the rotation frequency, and place a limit on the number of times your ad can be shown in a given time period. Why would you want this? Let's say that you have a strong ROI and too many impressions send you too much business. You can set a cap so you don't get 100 calls to your one-man business within 20 minutes after the ad begins.

Figure 8.12

Next is the hard part – trying to decide what you want your AdWords ad to say as shown in Figure 8.13. If you don't have experience with this, you should get professional help. It is another absolute science to determine the words that draw people to click on one ad versus another. It is industry specific.

Figure 8.13

Next is the keywords. Now you may want to just use the ones you decided in Chapter 2, but you can supplement them with other keywords, even if they have a lot of competition. Keep in mind, though, that some of these keywords can be pricey and you might want to do some research using the Google's Keyword Tool we also talked about in Chapter 2. In figure 8.14, you can see where to enter your keywords. Be sure to add them one per line.

Keywords

☐ Select keywords
Your ad can show on Google when people search for the keywords you choose here. These keywords will also automatically find relevant sites on the content network to show your ads. Start with 10 to 20 keywords that relate directly to your ad. You can add more keywords later. Help me choose effective keywords.

Enter one keyword per line. Add keywords by spreadsheet

```
<Enter new keyword>
```

Estimate search traffic

Advanced option: match types

Important note: We cannot guarantee that these keywords will improve your campaign performance. We reserve the right to disapprove any keywords you add. You are responsible for the keywords you select and for ensuring that your use of the keywords does not violate any applicable laws.

Figure 8.14

In figure 8.15, you see where you enter in the maximum amount you wish to bid for first page placement of Google search results. Keep in mind that if you leave the spaces blank you are writing a blank check. You will automatically outbid your competition. It will add up quickly, trust me – especially for those competitive keywords.

Placements

⊕ Select managed placements

Ad group default bids (Max. CPC)

You influence your ad's position by setting its maximum cost per click (CPC). The max CPC is the highest price you're willing to pay each time a user clicks on your ad. Your max CPC can be changed as often as you like.

Search ⑦ $
Content: managed placements $
Content: automatic placements $
Leave blank to use automated bids. ⑦

💡 This ad group is incomplete. Before your ads can run, you must complete the following tasks: Create at least one ad. Add at least one keyword or placement.
Note: You can save this incomplete ad group and complete these tasks later.

Save and continue to billing   Set up billing later   Cancel new ad group

Figure 8.15

Next you have to fund your account by clicking "Save and continue to billing" as shown in Figure 8.15. Billing simply means that you provide Google with a credit card number that they can use to charge your monthly advertising costs.

I would like to say that once you fund the account, your ads will begin showing immediately. But that is not true. Typically it takes Google about 2-3 days to approve or reject your add based on the content of your add. Google wants the ad to contain no foul language or email addresses, as well as many other published and unpublished rules.

Once your ad is approved, it will start immediately. However, in my experience, you only get a few hundred impressions the first week or so before it really kicks in and starts working. So don't expect to start AdWords today and get calls tomorrow.

Monitoring Your Campaign

The Campaign Management tab is where you'll perform most of the tasks to manage your account and see the results of the money spent as shown in figure 8.16. This tab contains an overview of the campaigns that you have running, as well as links to an account snapshot, tools for managing your accounts, conversion tracking tools, and a web site optimizer.

		Campaign	Budget	Status	Clicks	Impr.	CTR	Avg. CPC	Cost	Avg. Pos.
			$2.00/day	Eligible	373	424,470	0.09%	$0.60	$225.17	6.7
			$1.00/day	Eligible	7	27,444	0.03%	$0.66	$4.64	8.2
		Total - all but deleted campaigns			380	451,914	0.08%	$0.60	$229.81	6.8
		Total - search			284	79,326	0.36%	$0.63	$178.21	8.2
		Total - content			96	372,588	0.03%	$0.54	$51.60	6.5
		Total - all campaigns	$3.00/day		380	451,914	0.08%	$0.60	$229.81	6.8

Figure 8.16

177

The Ad groups tab allows you to create groups for ad campaigns and see a more detailed look at the monetary settings, as shown in figure 8.17.

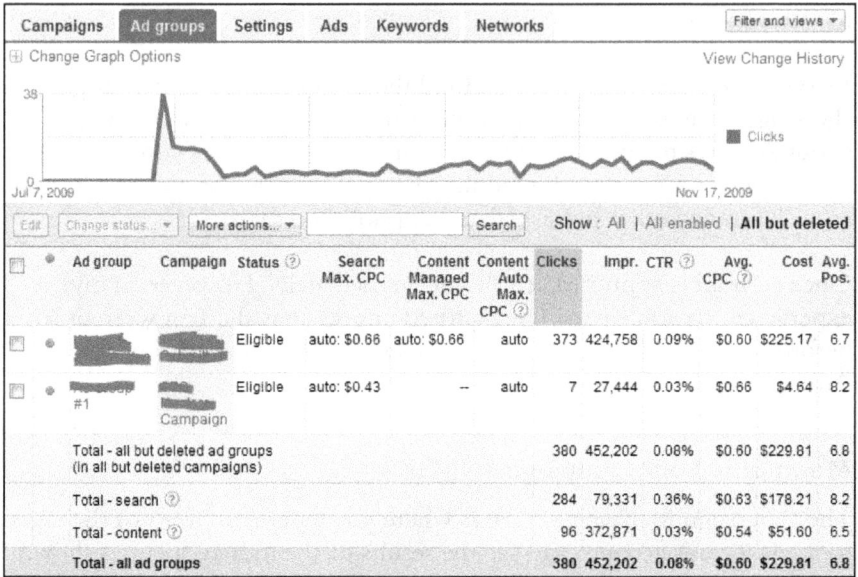

		Ad group	Campaign	Status ⑦	Search Max. CPC	Content Managed Max. CPC	Content Auto Max. CPC ⑦	Clicks	Impr.	CTR ⑦	Avg. CPC ⑦	Cost	Avg. Pos.
☐	•			Eligible	auto: $0.66	auto: $0.66	auto	373	424,758	0.09%	$0.60	$225.17	6.7
☐	•	#1	Campaign	Eligible	auto: $0.43	--	auto	7	27,444	0.03%	$0.66	$4.64	8.2
		Total - all but deleted ad groups (in all but deleted campaigns)						380	452,202	0.08%	$0.60	$229.81	6.8
		Total - search ⑦						284	79,331	0.36%	$0.63	$178.21	8.2
		Total - content ⑦						96	372,871	0.03%	$0.54	$51.60	6.5
		Total - all ad groups						380	452,202	0.08%	$0.60	$229.81	6.8

Figure 8.17

The Settings tab shown in figure 8.18 allows you to change all the settings that were displayed in figure 8.17. Simply click on any of the Budget options and it will allow you to change them.

The Ads tab shows the ads you have and how many clicks each ad received.

The Keywords tab allows you to see what keywords were clicked on and how many times they were shown. You can also change the keywords you are using by adding or removing them.

The Networks tab as shown in Figure 8.18, shows information on where your ad was click on and whether it was on Google.com or another one of their partner sites.

Figure 8.18

In the next few sections, let's take a look at the Reporting tab, the Billing tab, and the My account tab.

Reporting Tab

Click on the Reporting tab, and then choose Reports. You'll arrive at the Report Center screen, as shown in figure 8.19. You can see existing reports and the links to create new reports.

Figure 8.19

There used to be only three reports you could run: the Statistical, Financial, and Conversion reports. Google has come a long way, as you can see in Figure 8.20, which shows all the reports that are currently available. Each report is also customizable with many options.

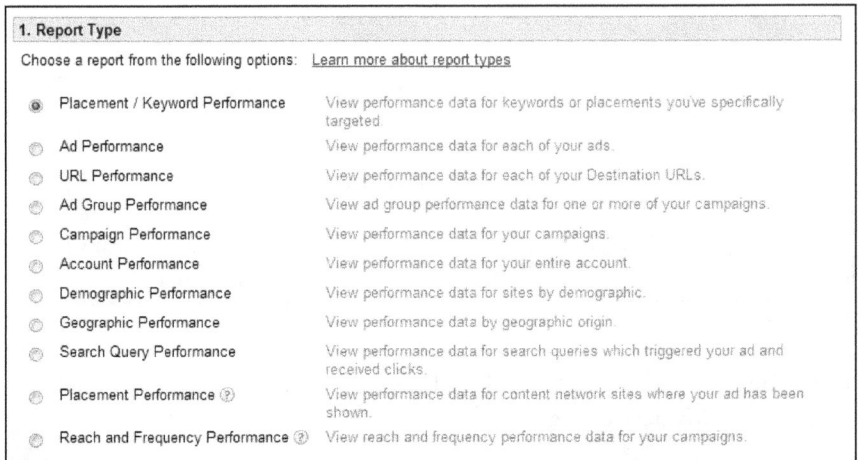

1. Report Type

Choose a report from the following options: Learn more about report types

●	Placement / Keyword Performance	View performance data for keywords or placements you've specifically targeted.
○	Ad Performance	View performance data for each of your ads.
○	URL Performance	View performance data for each of your Destination URLs.
○	Ad Group Performance	View ad group performance data for one or more of your campaigns.
○	Campaign Performance	View performance data for your campaigns.
○	Account Performance	View performance data for your entire account.
○	Demographic Performance	View performance data for sites by demographic.
○	Geographic Performance	View performance data by geographic origin.
○	Search Query Performance	View performance data for search queries which triggered your ad and received clicks.
○	Placement Performance ⑦	View performance data for content network sites where your ad has been shown.
○	Reach and Frequency Performance ⑦	View reach and frequency performance data for your campaigns.

Figure 8.20

Billing Tab

This tab allows you to keeping track of your invoices, billing information, account access, and account preferences.

This tab provides you with two options. Select either Billing Summary (which shows your payment type, the amount of the last payment, your current balance, and the current charges for each campaign), or Billing Preferences (which allows you to change the way you are billed or the credit card information on file).

My Account Tab

This tab allows you to change those Google accounts that can access your AdWords account and reports, as shown in figure 8.21. It also allows you to change your time zone, language, PhamacyChecker ID, or tracking options; get the Google AdWords terms and conditions; manage your business hosted page at Google Sites; or cancel your AdWords account altogether.

Account Access

If you manage this AdWords account with others, see who has access to sign in. Invite others to create their own login email and password to access this account by clicking 'Invite other users.' Learn more

+ Invite other users

Users with account access

Adwords user	Last logged in ⓘ	Access level ⓘ	Actions
	Nov 16, 2009	Administrative access	Actions ▾

Figure 8.21

Preferences

Preference for (sodom@surewest.net)

Language and number preferences Edit

Display language	ⓘ	**English**
Number format	ⓘ	**United States**

Account preference

Time zone

Time zone	**(GMT-08:00) Pacific Time**

PharmacyChecker ID

PharmacyChecker ID ⓘ	**No ID** Edit

Tracking

Auto-tagging	**No, thanks**

Google AdWords terms and conditions

Read printer-friendly document

Figure 8.22

This book isn't really about PPC campaigns and we just barely touched on Google AdWords. There is so much to learn.   Now let's take a look at the Microsoft AdCenter.

Adwords Tips

Don't Use geo-modified keywords in geo-targeted campaigns
This can result in a lot less traffic, since there is a strong chance the ads will not display due to a "geo-targeting mismatch."

Don't Duplicate keywords across ad groups or campaigns
When you have a good keyword, it may seem like a smart move to use them in all of your ad groups and campaigns. Duplicating your keywords won't help your performance. Your keywords will compete against each other and drive up your cost-per-click.

Don't rush to make bid changes
Making bid adjustments, pausing or deleting ads or keywords well before enough data has been collected to make an educated decision is just dumb. Wait until you have time and a baseline unless your budget is being eaten away too fast for little results.

Putting your phone number in your ad
This one may sound odd—why wouldn't you want to give your phone number? It might save a click. If you have a phone number in your ad people may call the number instead of clicking. This is good you think? No Google assigns a quality index score. If no one ever clicks on your ad it is shown less or will increase your cost-per-click to get your ad better results.

Copying a competitors ad
Doing this will could have legal consequences.

Choose "Match Phrase" whenever possible
Google likes to display an ad whenever you will let someone click it and pay money. If you choose "broad" Google may display the ad whenever any of the words are used in your keywords. That means if you sell fire alarms and someone types in "fire hoses" there is a good chance your ad will appear somewhere down the line and get clicked on. Even though the person has no intension of buying your product or service it will still get displayed.

Microsoft AdCenter

Microsoft AdCenter, formerly MSN AdCenter, is Microsoft's advertising program. PPC ads through Microsoft AdCenter are distributed on Bing, MSN, Live, Yahoo and many other smaller search engines.

Go to http://advertising.microsoft.com to setup an account, as shown in figure 8.23.

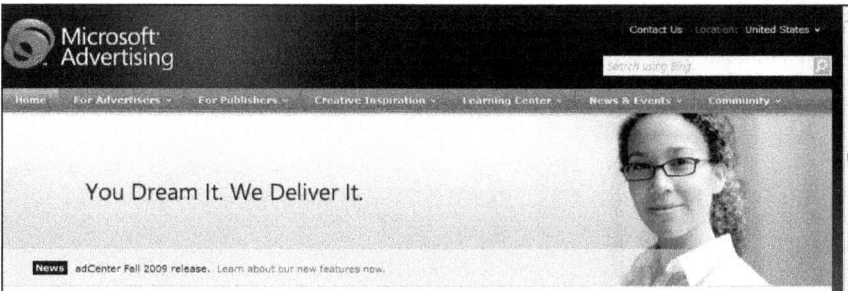

Figure 8.23

If you already have an account, go to https://AdCenter.microsoft.com, as shown in figure 8.24.

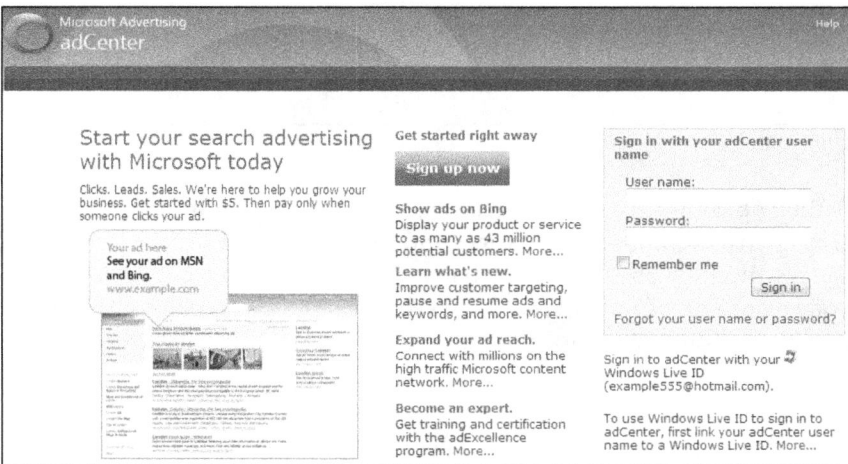

Figure 8.24

There is a new guide which explains all the new features of the Microsoft AdCenter: *http://advertising.microsoft.com/wwdocs/user/en-us/learningcenter/AdCenter_2009_Fall_Upgrade_Feature_Guide_US.pdf*

In figure 8.25, you see a list from Microsoft.com which explains the new features of the Microsoft AdCenter.

Top 5 Features

- **Search Query Performance Report**

  The Search Query Performance Report will pull reports that contain the actual queries that users perform that resulted in your ad being clicked. This report will provide you with information to help you manage your keyword lists by adding keywords that are aligned with actual user queries, in addition to identifying potential negative keywords to add.

- **Default Time Zone**

  The Default Time Zone feature will allow you to set a default or preferred time zone at the account level. Additionally, this feature will require a campaign level time zone to be selected in order to proceed with campaign creation if a default time zone has not been entered at the account level. This allows you to have the appropriate time zone aligned with every campaign.

- **Ad Preview Tool**

  The Ad Preview tool was added in advance of the Fall 2009 Upgrade, but it is being moved from the Campaigns tab to the new Tools tab with the fall upgrade. The Ad Preview tool assists you in confirming that your ads are showing on Bing without incurring unnecessary impressions or accidental clicks.

- **Agency Invitation and Termination**

  adCenter advertisers will be able to invite an agency to manage their adCenter account. When an advertiser invites an agency to manage their account, they will be inviting the agency to manage all of their accounts; there will be no capability to invite an agency to manage only specific accounts or campaigns.

- **Managing Multiple Accounts**

  The Customer Selection page included in the Fall 2009 Upgrade will ease the pain of agencies, SEMs and large organizations, and help them efficiently manage all of their accounts in adCenter.

Figure 8.25

Setting up your Microsoft AdCenter account is slightly different from setting up a Google AdWords account. One of the first differences is that Microsoft wants $5.00 and your billing information up front, even before you create a first campaign ad. The setup fee of $5.00 is charged to the credit card you provide for payment and charged immediately to your account.

Once you've provided billing information, you can begin to set up your first Microsoft AdCenter campaign ad. When you sign into AdCenter, you're taken to a general page that includes five tabs, which you can use to manage your AdCenter ads. These tabs are Home, Campaign, Accounts & Billing, Tools, and Reports as seen in figure 8.26.

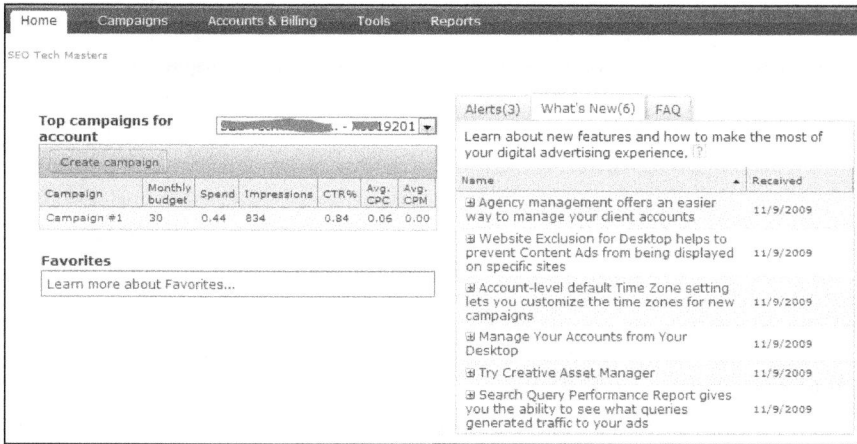

Figure 8.26

Home Tab

In figure 8.26, you see the Home tab which shows your campaigns, account information, Alerts, What's New and FAQ's.   This is the screen you see when you immediately go into your Microsoft AdCenter account.

Campaign

The Campaign tab in the Microsoft AdCenter (as shown in figure 8.27) is similar to the Google AdWords Campaign tab. When you click the Campaign tab, you're given an overview page, where you can create or import PPC campaigns. To create a campaign, click the Create Campaign button to start the creation process.

Figure 8.27

To keep you from getting bored, I am not going to walk you through the creation process because you are asked to provide all the same information that we just went through for creating a Google AdWords campaign.

One thing is a little different in the AdCenter campaign creation process, however: the importing capability is unique to the Microsoft AdCenter. Using this capability, you can import PPC ads that you've created in Microsoft Excel or another spreadsheet program. If the ads were not created in Excel, you need to save the file as a .csv file for importing.

Accounts & Billing Tab

The Accounts & Billing tab is where you'll find the financial information for your PPC accounts. From this page you have access to access and configure your company information, create a Business Page, configure users, change payment methods, get your billing statements and identify a client-agency relationship to identify a company that is handling your PPC campaign.

Tools Tab

The Tools tab is used for maintaining your PPC campaigns with research and other tools. The Tools tab in AdCenter gives you tools to help generate a keyword list, an ad Preview Tool to see what your ad will looks like, and a Microsoft Excel 2007 Add-in tool to create campaigns.

Reports

The final tab in the AdCenter console is the Reports tab. When you click the Reports tab, you're taken to the Create New Report page, where you can do just that. Once you've created a first report, it will appear on the Recent Reports tab with any other reports that you may have created.

You don't need to create a new report type each time you need to generate one. Simply save the report as a template; and then the next time you want to run a report, select the template during the report creation process. The list of reports you can create is shown in figure 8.28.

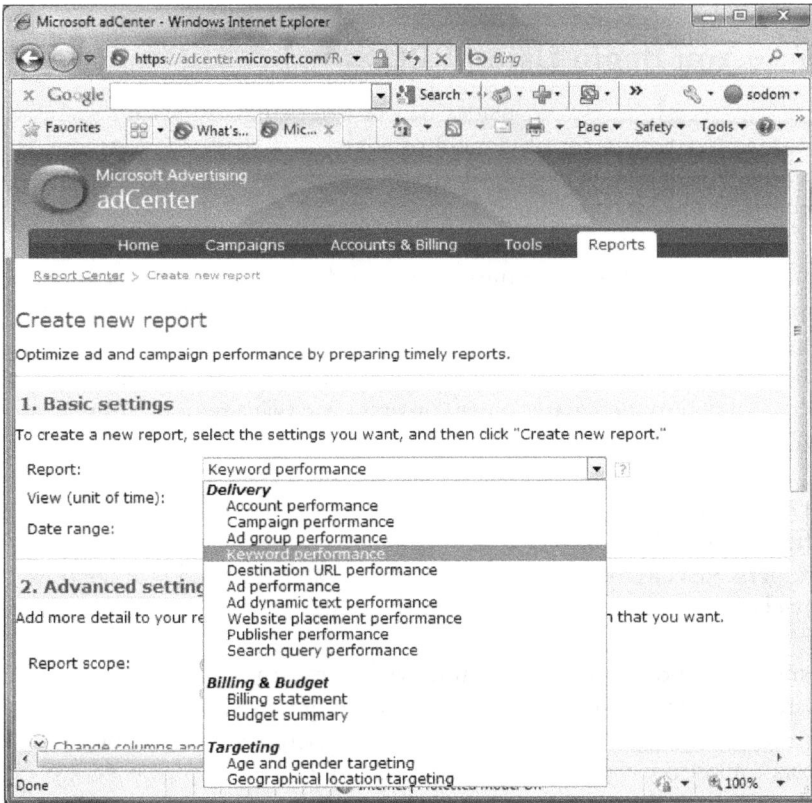

Figure 8.28

There are certain instances where Microsoft AdCenter can outperform Google AdWords, particularly since so many people formulate their marketing efforts toward Google and have not taken advantage of Microsoft's AdCenter.

Many organizations use more than one PPC campaign provider. Using multiple PPC vendors means better coverage with your PPC ad, which can lead to better conversion rates and a better ROI.

Before You Begin Using PPC

There are several things to consider before you being a PPC campaign. Because you're paying for placement or advertising space for your keywords, you're not necessarily going to get the best results with all the keywords or phrases that you choose.

In some cases you must continuously test and evaluate to see which keywords draw in the demographic that will buy your product or service. I recommend that you begin small, with a minimal number of keywords, to see how the search engine you've selected performs. You can also see the results and determine what it costs for first page placement of your sponsored ads.

You should also be able to gauge what it costs verses of the amount of traffic the ads deliver and how well that traffic converts into paying customers. Even if you make two sales you can gauge and average how many clicks it took to make a sale and the cost.

Having a method in place that enables you to track your return on investment is imperative. If your goal is to bring new subscribers to your web site, you'll want to track the conversions, perhaps by directing the visitors funneled to your site by your PPC link to a landing page set up just for them.

You can then monitor how many clicks came to that page in Google Analytics. This is easy to track if you have a special phone number or sales page setup for users coming from your PPC campaign. All this together will allow you to quickly track your ROI and to determine how much you're paying for each new conversion or sale.

Questions to Ask Before You Begin a Campaign

Before investing a lot of time and money into a PPC service, you may want to review a few different PPC Management services to determine which is the best one for you. If you choose to do it yourself you can gauge your readiness by seeing if you can answer these basic question:

1. How many searches are conducted each month through the search engine for which you're considering a PPC program for the keywords you have chosen?
2. What is the competition versus the number of searches for each keyword you have selected?
3. Does the search engine have major partners or affiliates that could contribute to the volume of traffic you're hoping to get?
4. How does the search engine or PPC program prevent fraudulent activity?
5. Is there recourse to get a refund or help with the investigation if click fraud occurs?
6. Do you know what to look for to determine if click fraud is occurring?
7. How difficult is it to file a report about fraudulent activity and how quickly is the issue addressed?
8. Do you have control over where your listing appears on the search engine?
9. Can you choose to have your listing withheld from affiliate searches or web sites?
10. Can you limit the amount you spend by day or by a particular search?
11. Do you know what your PPC campaign budget will allow?
12. Do you have time to learn PPC in depth?
13. Do you have the time to monitor your PPC campaign daily?

Some search engines and web sites have strict guidelines about how sites appear in their searches, on their web site, how partners and affiliates calculate visits, and how fraud is handled.

You need to think of these before you start. If you cannot answer the questionnaire with reasonable certainty that you can handle the task, it is more cost effective to have a professional run your PPC campaign.

If you are not up to the task, you could be stuck paying for clicks that didn't actually happen or are of no use and cost more than you can afford.

PPC Advertisement Text

The text of your PPC advertisement is the single most important element in determining the success or failure of your PPC campaign. Don't get confused. The optimization of your site for SEO and PPC advertising are two *separate* activities.

In fact the closest thing that ties them together are that they both use the same keywords. Choosing those keywords for both your SEO and PPC campaign does determine your success or failure in both.

Those chosen keywords should lead your targeted demographic (also known as qualified visitors) to your site through direct links. A successfully researched and implemented SEO strategy defines and optimizes your site for keywords relevant to the site topic that help visitors to find you by using search engines.

The combination of SEO and PPC ensures that your site is drawing *qualified visitors*. Once you understand the relationship between PPC and SEO, you can begin to consider what it takes to make PPC ads successful. It all starts with the right advertisement text.

In PPC you should never use category words which are broad. Category words are those that can relate to many things that your web site doesn't provide. Let's consider the example we used earlier where one of the keywords for the local gym was "exercise equipment." Well, that broad category keyword could get people to see your ad and click if they are trying to buy equipment or sell equipment or repair equipment. Want to pay for the useless click from those people?

Product words are more specific (think long-tail), and these are the words that people search for when they're ready to make a purchase. For example, keywords that make up a better long-tail word for the Tualatin Gym are "tualatin gym," "tualatin racketball," or "tualatin fitness center":

> ### Sidebar: Avoiding negative keywords
> *Negative keywords* are words that cause a PPC ad *not* to be shown. These are words that can be associated with the topic that you're targeting, but not with the specific product or service that you're trying to advertise.

For example, if your web site sells classical music, you should never use keywords such as country, heavy metal, or "rap." Most of the search engines are now smart enough to flag those words as negative keywords and reduce the number of times that your ad is shown.

It's important to keep your keywords grouped together if you are using different landing pages of your web site. It's these words that you'll be working with as you create your keyword advertisement text for each set of keywords.

> **Note:** *Using your keywords in your advertisement text can increase your advertisement click-through rates by as much as 50 percent.*

It always helps if you write down several clear sentences that express the message you want visitors to see. Just brainstorm and get the ideas written down. Make sure you include the benefits of your product or service as well. You should also write down several benefits that might draw in your searching demographic.

There is a way to cheat. See what words and phrases your competition are using by looking at their keywords on their web sites and looking at their ads posted on Google or Bing.

Writing Your Ad

Now that we have your list, we need to set the tone for the demographic we are looking for. For example, there is a big difference between the teenage generation and the senior generation. If you're trying to reach teens for video game sales, you'll want to write your advertisement in a language that attracts them. On the other hand, if you are trying to reach seniors, your slogan might be something more old-fashioned.

You shouldn't try to reach everyone with a single ad. If you do, you'll probably be reaching no one at all. Each demographic should have its own unique guidelines for ad text, and you should take the time to learn the requirements for the PPC campaign you need to create.

You should write and create your ad to be relevant and compelling. Here are some tips to help you:

- Include keywords in your ad text.

- Tell your potential visitors exactly what you offer and why they want it.
- Don't exaggerate claims regarding the benefits of your products or services.
- Create a sense of urgency if possible. Such as "Discount today only," "limited availability," or "offer expires soon."
- Draw valid demographics, not views. The purpose in PPC advertisement is to draw potential visitors to your site, not just get clicks.
- Use long full sentences and abbreviate when possible. Try to cut only non-keywords.
- Use strong, motivating words – you'll have a very limited amount of space in which to write your ad.
- Experiment endlessly. If your PPC ad is perfect right out of the gate, it will truly be an anomaly. Trust me.

You'll likely find yourself readjusting the ad you create frequently because of changes in your products or services. Set aside at least an hour or two a day to put into your PPC ad campaign, especially in the beginning. Only through experimentation and testing can you achieve PPC success and not break the bank..

Getting the Most out of PPC

As a web site owner you are always trying to get new and old customers back to our site. We want those human visitors to come to our web sites and to buy what we are selling. To entice new customers to your web site you cannot rely on your site being on the top of the search engines with no competition all the time.

Having a consistent PPC campaign is essential. Not only that but you can target your PPC campaign toward many more keywords than you can optimize your site for and make changes quickly and effectively.

We have learned in this chapter the effectiveness of the PPC Model, which is the most popular advertising model. Pay-Per-Click is exactly what it sounds like. The advertiser bids on keywords and tells the advertising company that they will pay a certain number of cents or dollars for every click on the ad that you place on the search engine or its partner web sites.

There are more places for PPC advertising than you might think. All these web sites have advantages in one way or another and might be effective for your web sites advertising. Here are some web sites you might consider for your PPC budget:

http://adwords.google.com/
http://www.content.overture.com/d
http://www.411web.com/
http://www.7search.com/
http://www.abcsearch.com/
http://www.adbrite.com/
http://www.ask.com/
http://www.brainfox.com/
http://www.enhance.com/
http://www.kanoodle.com/
http://search.looksmart.com/
http://www.lycos.com/
http://advertising.microsoft.com/home
http://www.miva.com/
http://www.search123.com/
http://www.searchfeed.com/
http://turbo10.com/

> **NOTE:** *Yahoo no longer makes the list because they are now operated by Microsoft AdCenter.*

There are some disadvantages to PPC as opposed to organic SEO listings, including the high cost of bids for certain keywords, poor conversion rates on purchased clicks, and click fraud which we discussed earlier.

Impressions in Cost Per Thousands (CPM)

The Cost Per Thousand Impressions Model (CPM) is often associated with banner advertising, but can now be purchased for text ads as well. This type of advertising is available from these sources:

- http://adwords.google.com/
- http://www.realtechnetwork.com/
- http://www.joetec.net/

Generally, per click, CPM advertising is much cheaper than PPC. It's cheaper because its effectiveness is usually less. As with any other type of advertising, you need to track click-through and conversion rates to determine if the advertising is effective for your business.

How much cheaper is it? Well, using Google AdWords, you can sometimes buy CPM advertising for as little as $2 per 1000 impressions. The major appeal of CPM advertising is its perceived low-cost, with rates ranging between $2 – $3 per 1000 impressions. Watch out though. Google could have 10,000 impressions for popular keywords in two days.

Just make sure to keep an eye on your advertising budget. From firsthand experience, I can vouch that it may appear inexpensive, but in a short time it can add up quickly.

Pay-for-Inclusion Services

Another tool that you can use to get paid results on a search engine is a service known as *paid inclusion*. Sometimes this is also called *pay for inclusion (PFI.)* Similarly there is another term called *pay per inclusion (PPI)*. It is similar although there is a small difference between the two. PFI is a strategy whereby you pay a fee small fee to be included in a search index. This fee doesn't guarantee your ranking on the search engine. It's a simple flat fee that's usually paid annually.

PPI is a strategy in which you pay a small fee to have your web sites URL included on a search engine. There is a twist however. The fee that you pay for PPI is based on the number of clicks you receive as a result of that inclusion on the search engine. Again, PPI does not guarantee your ranking on the search engine. Your only guarantee is that you will be listed on a search. Moreover, that per-click fee can often be comparatively high, in the range of $.25 to $.50 per click to your web site.

Click Fraud

Say you own a web site that allows Google AdWords to appear on the site. Knowing you make a profit the ads are clicked on, you go to the site whenever possible and click on the ads. Cha-ching! Money in your pocket. This would be what is known as click fraud.

Sometimes click fraud happens when a person, group of people, or automated script clicks on PPC advertisements. Because the concept of PPC is that advertisers pay each time someone clicks on their ads, this drives the cost of ads higher and higher without resulting in any conversions.

Sometimes there is no immediate monetary benefit. For example, your competition might do it just to make your costs higher. Some advertisers also believe that PPC providers commit and even encourage click fraud to drive profits. This might not be so far from the truth. Several court cases have resulted in settlements when PPC providers such as Google and Yahoo! were sued for contributing to or allowing click fraud.

Unless all the clicks come from the same IP address, it's hard to prove that click fraud is actually happening. There are many software programs, called clickbots, that can create clicks from what appear to be spoofed or different IP addresses.

In many cases, there are indicators of click fraud such as an inflated number of clicks without conversions, clicks that all occur from the same IP, the same city, or if the time of clicks is unusual. These can all be signs of click fraud.

Another good indicator for me is when the level of clicks from Google partner sites is more than half the number of clicks on the actual Google web site. That is a big red flag for me and when that starts happening I know to turnoff the ads on affiliate web sites.

If you suspect that you're being targeted by click fraud, immediately contact the fraud department of your PPC provider. If you don't receive satisfactory results from reporting the activity, then you should consider pursuing some type of legal action or discontinue the ads that are suspect.

Click fraud in the end can cost your company thousands, even tens of thousands, of dollars and ultimately destroy your PPC advertising campaign altogether. Only close monitoring of your stats for any signs of click fraud will help prevent it.

Look at this chart in figure 8.29. Because of constant monitoring we picked up on what appears to be an automated click fraud on day two of the fraud. Look at the figure. Can you tell the day?

Figure 8.29

We noticed the day this happened right away. We went to Google to see where they were all coming from and it was several affiliate web sites. It was easy to see the huge increase in clicks. Halfway through the next day we eliminated the problem. It hurt initially but at least we didn't go bankrupt not knowing the problem was there.

Click Fraud Is a Crime

Click fraud is a crime, whether you are falsely inflating the number of click-throughs on PPC ads either for personal gain or simply as a way to harm the competition.

In an effort to insulate themselves from criminal charges and to create as many problems as possible, some advertisers will employ what are called "clickbots." These are software programs that search for and click on PPC links to drive up prices. These "clickbots" are usually automated and very often almost impossible to trace back to their owners.

Another form of click fraud are called "Paid-to-Read" searchers, also known as PTR's. Businesses actually hire readers to read and click through PPC ads online. It's much harder to track multiple individuals than to track a single individual at one location using repetitive activity or "clickbots" to commit click fraud.

Search engines are being made to answer for click fraud, and the associated costs that PPC users are having to pay because of it, causing search engines to crack down on the problem. If you get caught conducting a click-fraud scheme, you could face stout fines and possibly even a criminal prosecution that could result in jail time.

Now that your head is about to explode with all this information on PPC campaigns, let's switch gears and look at how link building can help rankings in the next chapter.

Chapter 9 - Link Building

Link building is one of the biggest SEO tasks and where a good SEO guru shines. You can get your website to a Google PageRank of 2 without links, but after that your site needs to become relevant to the search engine with many links from sites that are in the same industry, industries related to your website, schools, or news organizations.

There is a reason that search engines care about links to and from your website. Remember our imaginary point system from the early chapters? The search engines treat your incoming links from other relevant websites a "point" for your site. The more you have the better. Some sites give you more points. News outlets such as DailyTrib.com, LocalNewsDay.com and CNN.com seem to help your rankings increase faster when you link to an from them. Other sites that give more points are .EDU and .Gov websites that provide links to your website.

> **TIP:** *Angela's and Paul's Backlinks Newsletter has been the standard for white hat link building. Every quarter they publish a list of where you can get free links from highly ranked websites.*
>
> *It runs about $99 per year but it is worth it. Virtually every SEO company subscribes to the newsletter. You can subscribe at: www.AngelasAndPaulsBacklinks.com.*

Just to give you a little history, once webmasters figured out that links helped your rankings, all sorts of abuse started to occur. People started creating ways to beat the system including link farms, massive reciprocal link networks, automatically generated content with automatic links, and automated software that automatically posted to thousands of links on the Internet. Most of these links were never meant for a human visitor to see.

This is where the major search engines began to fight back. They didn't want junk in their results any more than searchers wanted to see it. Search engines started counting some links more than others, and discounting some links and types of links entirely. Then they started to ban websites for using these practices.

Now, link building is no longer a simple "more equals better" formula and the mathematics behind search results has gotten much more complicated. Meanwhile, the ability to use "right link building" has actually gotten a lot easier.

Right And Wrongs Of Linking

If your linking strategy is accomplishing the items in the Right Link

Building column below in Table 9.1, you're heading in the right direction with your website linking.

How Link Building Affects...	Right Link Building	Wrong Link Building
Your Potential Visitors	Links that lead to good relevant content.	Links to content not meant for human eyes or deceiving content.
Search Engines	Links that improves search engine result quality.	Link that cause human visitors frustration and are unhelpful.
You	Links that are relevant and target your websites demographic, gives your website relevancy in your business or industry and ads credibility.	Links that don't drive relevant traffic to your website make your site seem cheap, fake, spammy or don't provide information related to the keywords used to find the site.

Table 9.1

Places To Get Good Website Links

There are an infinite number of places you can get good links to your website that are relevant and will increase the your rankings. These are:

1. Websites in your industry (Experts, your suppliers, wholesalers, industry regulators, Industry training and certification sites.)
2. Charity websites, educational institutions, places you sponsor
3. Chambers of commerce, BBB, Industry associations
4. Old sites with established domains
5. News organizations
6. Press release sites
7. Blogs and forums
8. Quality news articles
9. Websites from .gov and .edu sites
10. Social media and bookmarking sites
11. Customer review websites
12. Anyplace that you feel will bring you positive and relevant branding to enhance your company's credibility.
13. Links found in Angela's and Pauls Backlinks Newsletter. **www.AngelasAndPaulsbacklinks.com**

Tips For Creating Links

Anchor text is the visible, clickable text of a hyperlink (also known as link text). For example, if this were a website, then in this sentence, this would be the anchor text You don't always have control over your anchor text. If someone links to you from their blog, or someone writes an article about you, the writer may not give you "keyword friendly" anchor text. In those cases, just be happy they linked to you. But, in other cases, you may be able to choose your anchor text.
Search engines pay particular attention to the anchor text that they are following. So, for your anchor text, use descriptive keywords and anchor text variants under which you would like to rank.

For example, if you own the site welding, you would want your anchor text . Especially when your text has your companies name in it and link it to your website. You need to vary your anchor text. Search engines view the links as more natural when you vary the anchor text. So, you don't want to use a link to your websites homepage every time your company name is mentioned. If they then talked about TIG Welders you might create a link that goes only to TIG Welders on your website or another.

> **NOTE:** *You should remember to use variants of singulars and plurals, your company name, and your website name.*

Build Links from Different IP Addresses

Now, if you're not link spamming, you probably don't have to worry about this one. But, if you are purchasing large amounts of links from questionable sources, and they say they'll put your links on 100's of unique domains, chances are they own all these domains. If they own all of these domains, then the domains are probably clustered on the same static IP address (The IP address of the server they host all their websites on.) Having a large number of links from the same IP address can be a warning sign to the search engines.

Link Juice

The term "link juice," refers to the voting power that a link passes to a page to which it links. The fact is only Google knows exactly how much link juice is getting passed on from each link on a page. However, there are some basic factors we can use to determine how valuable a given link will be. Looks for links with these quality for better results:

- The page is relevant to your content.
- The link from the page to your page has good anchor text.
- The other outgoing links on the page look relevant and appear to be to quality sites.
- The text around the link that you will receive is relevant. The page has been recently cached by Google recently within the month. To check the cached date please see the instructions in Chapter 1.
- The page is a respected or authority page such as a charity, news, educational or government website.

The Orphan Page Link Test

An orphan page is a page that has no links from any other page and hence cannot be found by search engines. If you want to test if Google learns links. Please a link to the orphan page.

The next time Google indexes your page with the link to the orphan page, check to see if the orphan page was indexed by the search engines. If your orphan page gets indexed by Google, then there is a good chance the page you are testing is passing on link juice.

Linking Within Your site

It's easy to focus only on inbound links, but there are important best practices for linking within your site as well:

> **Site maps** – Have one. If not for your visitors, for search engines. It's rough for search engines to have to drill down and find all that content. Make it easy for them. Oh, and keep it updated!

> **Anchor text within content** – This may be even more important for onsite links that for offsite links. You have

full control of your anchor text, so use it. Plus your site theme is already in place, so each link will have complete, natural relevance to the page it points to.

Breadcrumbs – Are a little piece of search engine love. Breadcrumbs are not only helpful for navigation, but search engines can pick up great anchor text from them. Breadcrumbs are the navigation elements that large sites use to help categorize content, and allow you to find your way back to core categories if you lose your way.

Featured products, news, etc. – Links from your homepage are, in general, considered more important than links from other parts of your site. So if you've got something you really want to show off, it makes sense to put it on your homepage, not only for usability, but for search engines as well.

Links to yourself – Link to your product or service pages from your own blogs, articles, resource sections, news releases, or any other relevant pages. Use the anchor text within each of these resources to send a little link love to your core pages. So, for example, if you sell toothbrushes, and you write a blog post about correct brushing practices, link the word toothbrushes from your blog post to your main toothbrush product page.

Directories

A directory is not a search engine, although the two types of sites are sometimes confused. A search engine finds its content by "crawling the web" via little roving programs called search engine spiders or robots.

A directory works completely differently than a search engine. A directory does not find content. It waits for you to bring the content to it. You submit your site, a human editor reviews and approves the site, and the directory includes your site URL under a category link (real estate sites, writing sites, baseball sites, whatever).

Users can find sites by drilling down through categories and viewing lists of related sites. Many directories are *search*able, but that does not make them *search* engines.

Directories have been around for a long time, and submitting your site to directories used to be all the rage in search engine optimization. You'll still find plenty of services out there advertising that they'll submit you to 1000's of directories. But like all SEO practices that have been overdone, mass directory submission doesn't work like it used to. That doesn't mean, however, that directory submission is dead. It just means that you have to do your due diligence before submitting to directories. Some of the directories I suggest are:

- Best of the Web – botw.org
- Librarians Internet Index - www.lii.org
- Yahoo Directory – directory.yahoo.com
- Business.com
- Jayde.com
- Open Directory — dmoz.org
- Joe Ant — joeant.com
- Starting Point – stpt.com/directory

Social Bookmarking Sites

To get your links on social bookmarking sites, all you have to do is create a profile and post them. That part is pretty easy. Getting people to bookmark or vote for your links can be the tricky part.

To get people to bookmark or vote for your links, you need to be patient, and you need to be active on your chosen bookmarking site(s). Find other people with similar interests and colleagues that you already know. Share their links. They'll be more likely to pay attention to and vote for your links in turn.

Popular bookmarking sites include:

- del.icio.us - The oldest social bookmarking website and most popular. Users can also add people to their networks and share bookmarks.

- StumbleUpon.com – Has a browser add-on for saving and sharing websites. Works with IE, and Mozilla.

- Mister-wong.com - One of my personal favorites. The layout is nice looking and user friendly. Allows you to import/export.

- Digg.com - Digg allows you to submit stories, then digg users can "Digg" the stories, and make comments. Users can also upload videos, images and podcasts.

- Propeller.com - A social news and bookmarking portal that's part of the AOL network. Stories are submitted to specific channels, and then voted on by members.

- Simpy.com - Allows users to save, tag and search bookmarks, attach notes, and browse other user's links. Links can be public or private.

- Diigo.com - Allows users to bookmark, highlight parts of web pages, tag, add notes, and create and join groups. Diigo is also a collaborative research tool.

- Sphinn.com - Social bookmarking site for marketers. Allows you to share news, articles, etc., and participate in discussions

Buying Links

This is definitely an example of what not to do. The major search engines do what they can to make sure a website's popularity is not increased by the use of paid links or link farm.

Buying links from sites that are very relevant to your website though will help you. If you've developed a reputable brand, a few paid or sponsored links could help drive traffic, and they are highly unlikely to hurt your rankings. When buying links, here are few things NOT to do:

- **DON'T** buy links from unrelated or poor quality sites.
- **DON'T** buy too many links at once. Make sure your link building looks natural (plan it out over time).
- **DON'T** purchase links from someplace that you wouldn't want to be associated with.
- **DON'T** purchase links from a page with a ton of other links on the page – try to keep the number of links on the page under 10.

The Future of Link Building

Finally, I'd like to leave this chapter on link building with a note on a very crucial concept that I believe will be imperative to future link-building efforts called "page segmentation".

Page segmentation has been a topic of long discussion, and the term is traditionally grounded in the way humans naturally segment and digest a web page. That is, humans can discard a repeating footer as a boiler plate. We know that anything in the top left-hand corner is probably pretty important; and if it's in a banner, we'll look at it if we get around to it.

Typically if it's part of the site template, we more or less ignore it, unless we need to look at it for navigation. Within a few seconds, we can tell where the core content is of a web page and where the ads are. From there we judge which content is important to us and what is not.

Google and Bing have been working very hard to develop new algorithms that digest pages much like humans do. They are making great strides and just like humans, search engines will have good instincts soon. Search engines themselves will be able to better discount links that are in ads (typically those that appear on the right side of a web page) as less important than other links because the links don't occur within actual content blocks. They'll be able to tell whether a link is spammy because it doesn't match the content on a page or a link is simply part of a site that covers several different topics.

The result is this. More than ever, you'll have to build your link campaigns on common sense. Stay with what's good for the user and for your site without worrying about search engines and avoid templates and spammy type ads and links.

Helpful Link Building Resources

Here are the simple search engine specific commands to find out which links each search engine finds relevant for your web site:

- **Google** - "+www. examplesite.+com" -site:www. examplesite.com

- **Yahoo** - linkdomain:examplesite.com —examplesite.com

- **Bing** - link: examplesite.com or inbody: examplesite.com

Toolbars and Add-ons:

SearchStatus (quirk.biz/searchstatus/) – Browser add-on for Firefox and Mozilla that shows a variety of information about a site or page including backlinks, PageRank, Alexa Rank, mozRank and Compete Rank.

SEOBook SEO Toolbar – (tools.seobook.com/seo-toolbar/)

SEOMoz.org Tools

- **Linkscape™** provides a variety of link data. - seomoz.org/linkscape (free)
- **Backlink Analysis Tool** - seomoz.org/backlink-analysis (paid)

Juicy Link Finder – helps you find links with authority and domains with high PageRank.

Backlink Analysis Tools

- backlinkwatch.com
- tools.seobook.com/backlink-analyzer

Anchor Text Analysis
- webconfs.com/anchor-text-analysis.php
- linkdiagnosis.com

Google Webmaster tools - google.com/webmasters/tools

Yahoo Site Explorer - siteexplorer.search.yahoo.com

Chapter 10- SEO Planning and Goal Setting

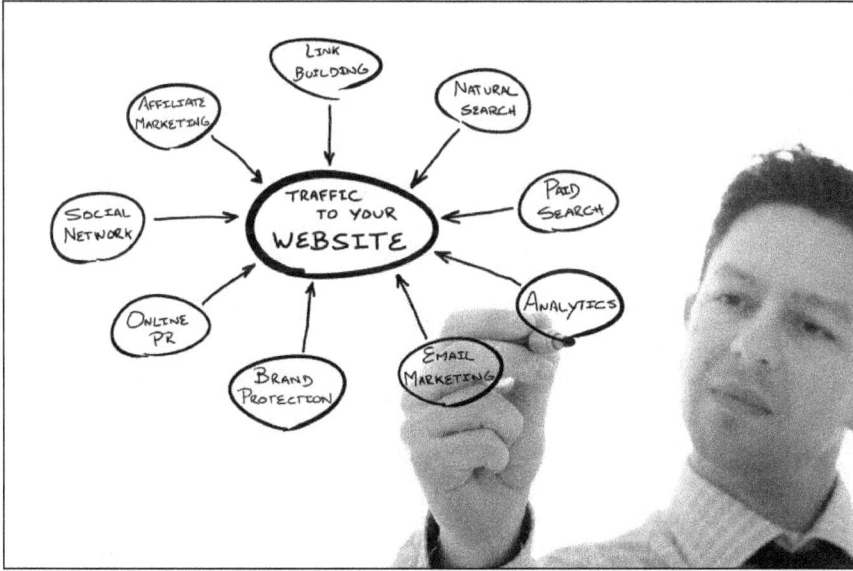

For most people the goal is simple, outdo what your competition does for the same keywords and beat their rankings. So I guess the chapter is done. Well, maybe it's not that simple. Maybe I should break it down just a little.

Before we begin, you should have a search engine optimization plan in place. This will help you create your SEO goals. Your SEO plan should be updated every 3 months based on what your competition is doing versus what your previous changes have accomplished. You will need to look at web site analytics which will help you understand where your needs are at as well as how your hits to conversion ratio is working. This will also help you see where you need to concentrate your efforts at any given time.

Before reading this chapter, however, you should have a good understanding of your trophy keywords and the other keywords you want to focus on. If you don't, you should visit Chapter 2 and make sure you know the keywords your company needs to use and the competition that is competing for those keywords.

In the beginning, you're most likely going to be focusing your SEO on getting your site listed on all the search engines. For this part, Chapter 3 should be your first stop. If you haven't done all the steps outlined in Chapter 3, then you should stop now and jump back there and make sure that your web site's URL is listed on all the hand submissions and you have your web site being submitted through automation to all the other smaller search engines and directories.

By now you should be familiar with the focus of the other chapters. We have already talked about adding your keywords into the content of each page and making each page focused on one subject, getting relevant links to your web site, adding keywords to the content of each page, adding Meta tags, adding correct titles with keywords, adding multimedia, adding social media, and providing the correct word density on each page for a focused search engine.

Each one of these components is a must on your web site and is all a part of your SEO strategy. These are all a part of your SEO plan and all of these components are an "add it once and forget about it" type of deal. You need to continuously monitor what is working, what is not, what your competition is doing, and make adjustments as necessary to maintain and update the elements of SEO that help you rank well.

The basic rule here is that your efforts will change, but they will never end. You need to plan to continue using, modifying, and updating your web site to help your SEO rankings, and changing your strategies based on search engine changes, new internet components, etc.

For instance, last year having Twitter and RSS feeds on your web site did virtually nothing for rankings. The year before having a YouTube video on your web site did almost nothing for rankings. This year they are an absolute must-have to increase rankings.

This year a major change took place. Bing didn't even exist last year and our recommendation was to focus your SEO strategies only on Google with a Yahoo! as an afterthought. Now because of all the changes, you might actually get more business by optimizing for Bing than your ever realized. Bing has a major market share now. With a majority of the web site optimized for Google and not Bing, there is market share to gain by optimizing for Bing, especially in the very competitive keyword arena where the competition is higher than most for a keyword.

Today, every major search engine focuses on many components of a web site in ranking a web site. This means that over time, if you are focused only on a single keyword or links, you will find that your SEO efforts will begin to fail quickly.

You have to keep your efforts up and not let down your guard. You can spend a year getting your web site's rankings high and be on the first page for any search with your keywords only to lose everything in a week. The fact is you can spend months getting your rankings up and they can be lost in a fleeting moment if you are not careful.

Let me give you an example. There is a very large software company that I do the SEO for. I spent a year and a half getting them to a Google ranking of 8 out of 10. It was one of my most prized accomplishments and I jumped for joy and bragged to everyone I worked with the day I looked and their web site ranking was an 8/10 on Google. Only a month later they were a 2. So what happened?

Someone took over their web site development who didn't have a clue about SEO. The new designer worked with the owner of the company to create a flashy new web site without any consultation from me. In fact, my point of contact with the company didn't even know it was being done. The new web site was all Flash and looked great.

The trouble is that when it was created, none of my SEO work was incorporated into the web site. Even worse, the new web designer changed all the page file names for every page that was indexed with the search engines. So when users on the search engines searched on their keywords and clicked on a link to their web site, there was no page. Rather, there was an error saying the page didn't exist. They were now invisible on the internet. Sales dropped to all time lows in a single month. It was two weeks before someone at my office noticed what was going on and contacted the company. By then it was too late.

When you went to their "About Us" page that used to be named "aboutus.html" it went to an error page because the new web developer named the file "about_us.php". This happened four months ago and they have reverted back to the old site as the SEO work I did would have been lost on the new page names. Search engines don't like web sites that change their page names all at once but they like the content to change frequently. The indexed pages weren't there anymore causing the search engine to drop the already ranked and indexed pages. Not only that, but links to the pages from other sites that gave them the rankings all lost ranking points because now they had broken links as well.

Today, the software company web site that was once on the first page of every major search engine for their keywords is on page 3 of Google and has a ranking of 4/10. Their sales went from averaging 150-200 sales per month to only 63 last month. This was a catastrophe for them. They were on an uphill trend adding new employees and growing all because of the SEO work I was doing for them. Today they are four employees fewer and just barely staying in business. I do have them climbing back up but it is slow going.

A web site needs constant growth and relevant material constantly to maintain its good rankings and keep the site from becoming what is known to search engines as a stale web site (a web site where the material never changes.) Those changes, however, need to be looked at from an SEO optimization perspective from every angle. Most outsiders think that every web designer is familiar with SEO. From my experience, very few have any knowledge of it. It is a specialization that most web designers and developers know little or nothing about.

So what should your SEO Plan include? Let's look at this in the next section.

Time and Effort in an SEO Plan

The first thing your plan needs to include is lots of time. Then add more time to that. This is one of the main reasons that most companies sub out their SEO work. Not only because it takes someone who lives and breathes SEO to keep up on the latest trends and technology, but because of the amount of time involved.

Simply adding new content here and there on your web site and changing a Meta tag or two won't help you increase your rankings on the major search engines.

> **NOTE:** *If you are doing the SEO yourself, to keep pace and save some time, you might consider designing your site similar to a blog where content is easily changeable.*

Your SEO plan should be considered a dynamic document that changes all the time based on your needs assessed from monitoring not only your web site, but the search engines and your competition on the search engines. If you can't figure out what your competition is doing to one up your SEO work, then you need to call in a professional and you need to do it fast because what you do today has virtually no effect on search engines for months. In essence, you are planning today what you want to happen on the search engines 3-6 months from now. An SEO plan will help you stay on track.

Now that you understand how important it is to put time into your web site's SEO, we need to create a clearly defined goal built around your business needs. Virtually every business has different needs and at different levels even when two different company web sites are in the same industry.

A small local business would focus only on the local area long-tail keyword searches, whereas a large business selling nationally or in a large geographical area would need to invest time, money, and considerable effort into increasing the exposure of their web site to potential customers outside its geographic region on a larger level using more generic shorter keywords.

For example, if you sold sports equipment in Orlando, you would target a local campaign using the keyword of "Orlando sports equipment." If your web site sold sports equipment nationally you would target a much harder keyword with more competition such as, "sports equipment". The fewer the words, the harder it is to get your site listed higher in the search engines. The broader the keyword, the more competition there is for that keyword.

In Orlando there are probably 30 web sites competing for sports equipment and maybe ten percent do any professional search engine optimization. However, nationwide there are probably thousands vying for first place on the search engines with those broader keywords. If only one percent do search engine optimization, you have a lot of competition to beat to one up all those other companies.

Both the smaller company and the larger company need to implement an SEO plan. The larger company that needs to concentrate on a national level with lots of competition will require more than this book can offer (unless you are just starting your web site). If you are trying to do a national campaign with lots of competition, most likely your competition is employing powerhouse professional help. This is not the time to experiment.

Your revenue (The money you make from your web site) is an important factor. Your SEO plan and goals should not only focus on increasing your web site visits, but also on increasing your revenues. You can track revenue by funneling your web site visitors through individually targeted sales transaction pages while they are visiting your web site.

You should make sure the goals you set are realistic. It's very easy to become unfocused with your SEO efforts and get discouraged when those efforts don't meet your goals or expectations. It's very easy to spend gobs of money on SEO and never accomplish anything.

Your SEO goals and the plan you create must be flexible and grow with your organization.

SEO Plan Details

Now that you have a set of goals in mind for your web site, it's time to create an SEO plan. The SEO plan is the document that you'll use to help you stay focused as you try to implement your individual SEO strategies.

Keyword Research

Continuous keyword research should be your second line item after your time entry on your SEO plans details. Google Analytics has a way of looking to see what keywords were used to find your site. Many times it becomes clear that there are a market of people who find your site that you didn't even know.

I will give you an example. My SEO web site targets many keywords, but I noticed that several people searching for better web site rankings searched using the keyword "search engine help" and found my web site way down on the list of a search engine. After a few of these in one month, I added the keyword to my PPC campaign. After getting about 80 hits from that in one month, I optimized a landing page just for that keyword. I now get about 200 hits per month from that term which is business I never would have gotten had I not been analyzing the keywords people were using to access my site.

It was a minor change in the bigger picture. I was already creating content for the site, but by focusing on some of the most logical and well known keywords. I didn't crawl in the mind of a prospective searcher but Google caught it for me. I just had to interpret the results.

You should never discount the little things. Even minor details, such as refocusing and changing your keyword efforts or modifying the tagging on your pages can have a major impact if it is done right. For every web site that I do SEO, I find a little niche on a monthly basis that my clients' competition never catches and I capitalize on that. Using those little niches in the right places can make a major difference in the amount of traffic that your site receives.

Reputation Management

The next item you should have in your plan is reputation management, which is a critical part of any online business. If you Google anyone of my SEO client's URL's, you see nothing but good press. The top 10 results of a search are usually corporate sites, blogs, press releases and other landing pages I optimized or created for them. This is no accident. Many clients who do any volume of online sales will get a disgruntled customer or two and sometimes a negative a news article or other problem can affect their online reputation.

Sometimes this bad press is known when it comes out in a news article that everyone sees and talks about. Sometimes, however, a disgruntled person can place negative information on blogs, as comments, and many other places that can be indexed into the search engines and work to destroy your online presence little by little. If you do not take time to monitor you SERP (Search Engine Results Page), you may miss the reason you are dropping in sales or hits to your web site because of the negative that is displayed. In one case I had a customer who owned a large mortgage company. Their company does about 8,000 loans per year and have to turn down some clients for a loan, often at the last minute because of some unforeseen issue such as the client used a credit card or bought a car and dropped their credit scores, disqualifying them for the loan product for which they had been approved. It is inevitable, like it or not they have gained a few disturbed clients and they occasionally post their negative comments. On this occasion they managed to fill up four of the top ten spots on a Google search for many of their important keywords.

Then the inevitable happened. The web visits stopped and the phone calls stopped coming. This is a good example of what can happen if you don't have monitoring your online reputation a part of your SEO plan. You're probably saying, this is nice to tell me but where do I start if I find negative links or information about my company?

Before this ever happens, you should identify key editorial contacts at industry and business publications, EZines, and press release portals that can help to place positive press in its place. Make a separate page in your plan to log these contacts. You should always be looking for opportunities to post comments on relevant articles and place links to your company's URL.

Today, you can publish stories in minutes, versus days, weeks or months. So when you do post content, it not only appears on the Web site, but on search engines, syndicated content sites, and news search engines as well.

You should always create targeted press releases that can be linked-to from a variety of sources. The press release should also be optimized for the best relevant keyword density so it appears as high as possible in related searches. If you skipped learning about keyword density, there is an index in the back of this book. I would recommend learning about how to use that to your advantage.

Launch your own blog and become friendly with other bloggers, because bloggers are the most publicized arm of social online media. Bloggers are increasing their credibility with the consumer, which means their opinions really do matter. This is somewhat like a "Third Party Endorsement." Having bloggers post negative comments about you or your brand can spell disaster. Be prepared to get into the conversation by posting comments on blogs with negative content about your product/services and link back to your own press release or blog.

Another very effective tool is the use of sub-domains. Google sees them as separate web sites, but they do still carry the authority and trust of the root domain. When you create a sub-domain, you must not simply copy content from your main domain. The content must be different. The new sub-domain must have useful, unique content. It does not need 100 pages; just ten or so pages per sub-domain will do. All you need is two to three well-optimized sub-domains.

Sign up for a Twitter account and place the Twitter Wiki on your web site, but keep updating it with relevant information about your site. You might also consider MySpace and Facebook, or other social bookmarking network entries. And of course, post links to your press releases using keywords in your text links.

Managing your reputation requires the creation of relative content on your own web site, distribution of positive content, as well as strategic participation in online discussions. When you combine these strategies, an integrated search engine reputation management program is in place and ready for action in the event a negative piece of information is indexed about your company or URL.

PPC

Monitoring your PPC account is, of course, important. Whether you use Google AdWords or Bing's AdCenter or related pay-per-click programs to get your message out there you need to constantly monitor which keywords are working for you and which ones get a lot of clicks but don't turn into sales. Too broad of a keyword, as we learned in previous chapters, can cost you a lot of money with very little results. In terms of reputation management, a PPC campaign can help as well. While optimized press releases and related content may take days or weeks to appear high in relevant search results on search engines, paid text ads are virtually instantaneous and provide total control over placement (by keyword) of your message.

Reprioritizing Pages

In the beginning, prioritizing your web pages is easy. Give priority to the pages that focus on each of your keywords, and in the same order that your keywords are in. You should prioritize your efforts on the pages that support those trophy words and draw the most amount of traffic and sales.

These are top-priority pages and visitors should naturally gravitate to those pages. These should be focused landing pages that utilize all the optimization techniques, including social media and keyword density optimization. The content should remain relevant and constantly be updated so it never gets stale.

Pages such as your home landing page or those that will generate the most traffic or revenue should be a road map and included in your SEO plan and goals should be set for your marketing efforts. If four of the web pages on your site are your top priority, those should encompass a majority of your time and efforts in your SEO plan.

Additional Plan Items

After you have prioritized your sites web pages, you should assess where you stand and where you need to be with your current SEO efforts. Make a checklist and dedicate time to assess all the pages in your web site. Those that should be checked more frequently are the following:

- Keywords
- Keyword density
- Title tags
- Social media elements
- Site/page tagging
- Page content relevancy
- Replacement of stale content
- Frequently changed content
- Blogs
- Social media optimization
- Social bookmarking
- Site linking
- Press release writing
- Article submissions
- Video optimization
- RSS Feeds
- Search engine placement
- PPC

Items that can be checked less frequently:

- Site map accuracy
- Longevity of domain registration
- Robots.txt optimization
- Site map
- HTML source code and errors
- Alt tags
- Link development
- Manual link requests to related sites
- Directory listings
- One-way links/two-way links
- HTML design
- ASP. and other coding such as Java and Flash
- Linked URLs

Completing the Plan

At this point you should have collected all the information you need to put into your SEO plan. You should also have a good idea of the priority of each item and what needs to be done frequently and which ones can be done on a less frequent basis to increase or maintain your web site's search engine rankings.

Now it's time to put all of the information that you've gathered into a comprehensive plan comparing your available time and determining the SEO efforts you should be making to best utilize that time. Your SEO plan is more than just a simple picture of what's included in your web site and what's not. This is the document you should use to help determine your web site's current search engine rankings, reputation management, your needed marketing efforts, capital expenditures, time frames, and how you're going to keep your web site from becoming stale.

The plan should look much like a business plan when you are done. It includes your goals, a work plan, marketing information, how you will grow your business, plans for managing problems, and much more.

Those strategies can include efforts such as manually submitting your site or pages from your site to directories and planning the content you'll use to draw search engine bots, spiders, and crawlers. It should also outline which pay-per-click programs you plan to use and a time line for the testing and implementation of those efforts, as well as regular follow-ups.

I always recommend that you supplement your SEO with a well-managed PPC campaign. But the goal is to maintain your URL on the first page of a search engine's search using organic SEO to maximize those naturally occurring elements. When you build on each internal and external element on your web site to create a site that will naturally fall near the top of the search engine results pages (SERPs), you achieve high SERPs rankings free — other than the time it takes to implement your SEO plan.

Achieving each ranking point for organic SEO can take anywhere from three to eight months if you implement the right SEO plan. Don't get upset if you don't see immediate results from your SEO efforts. Stick to your SEO plan. If you don't see changes within 3-6 months or your rankings get worse, you should reevaluate your SEO plan or seek professional help.

Chapter 11-SEO Toolbars, Tools & Plug-Ins

If you search the internet you can find a plethora of SEO tools for sale. However, from experience I can tell you there is a free tool for just about everything. Not only that, but ninety percent of the tools that you have to pay for may also do the following:

1. Separate your money from your bank account.

2. Get information from you on how to contact you so someone from India,Pakistan, or some other far off land can hard sell you on their SEO services, tools, or whatever you're searching for at ridiculous amounts. I might add that there are some legitimate SEO services in Middle Eastern countries but you will find the fraudulent ones much easier. They usually contact you.

3. Con you into paying for SEO tools that many times are free.

4. Con you into paying for a tool that works worse than the free tool.

Lucky for you, you are reading a book by two authors who have pretty much been there and done that for all of the above. Be very skeptical of any SEO option not included in this book or on one of our blogs. In this book, we outline free alternatives that work just as well for every type of tool. Many of the times these free tools work better than the paid alternative.

This is the section in many other SEO books where I am very disappointed because endorsements for software galore are given and the free alternatives are left out. In fact while we were writing this book, we had a company offer to pay us $5,000 for an endorsement in our book for their analytics software and another offered us $2,500 for endorsing their SEO web site full of different SEO tools which are pay-per-use.

Both wanted us to leave out different free products, especially Google Analytics and Google Keyword Tools. Unfortunately for those web sites and software companies, we have our own reputation management to maintain and we decided early on to make this a true SEO reference guide and not endorse any paid product unless there wasn't a better free alternative. You can be assured that we have accepted no paid endorsement fees for this book and contracted that with the publisher. This means you can trust what we write.

In the next few sections I will be looking at many different toolbars, free plug-ins, extra buttons, and software and web site tools to help you with your SEO efforts. Let's start in the next section, called Toolbars and Plug-ins.

Toolbars and Plug-Ins

In site optimization and monitoring, browser toolbars are especially useful. Best of all, the ones you really need are free. In this section, I will talk about the Alexa Toolbar and go more in depth on what you can do with the Google Toolbar using plug-ins. If you did not read how to install the Google Toolbar in chapter 1, you should go back there and read that section first.

Since the Google Toolbar will encompass most of this section and has plug-ins to learn about, let's take a look at this first. Now I am assuming that you read and followed the instructions in Chapter 1 and already have the Google Toolbar installed with the PageRank icon sitting in the bar. Now, my Google Toolbar looks like the one in figure 11.1.

Figure 11.1

I bet your wondering what all these little icons in figure 11.2 are and how they got there. You're probably also asking yourself, "What do they do and how can they help me?"

Figure 11.2

Google has many plug-ins that can be accessed by pressing the "Adjust Toolbar Options" (the icon that looks like a wrench) on the Google Toolbar and selecting the Custom Tools option. When you do this you will see a screen similar to the one in Figure 11.3.

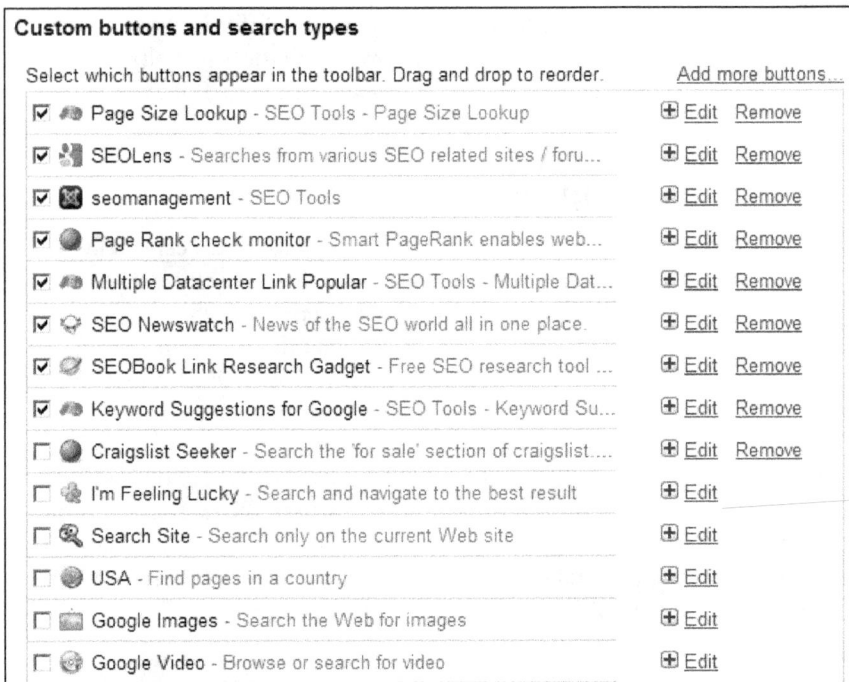

Custom buttons and search types

Select which buttons appear in the toolbar. Drag and drop to reorder.   Add more buttons...

☑ Page Size Lookup - SEO Tools - Page Size Lookup	⊞ Edit	Remove
☑ SEOLens - Searches from various SEO related sites / foru...	⊞ Edit	Remove
☑ seomanagement - SEO Tools	⊞ Edit	Remove
☑ Page Rank check monitor - Smart PageRank enables web...	⊞ Edit	Remove
☑ Multiple Datacenter Link Popular - SEO Tools - Multiple Dat...	⊞ Edit	Remove
☑ SEO Newswatch - News of the SEO world all in one place.	⊞ Edit	Remove
☑ SEOBook Link Research Gadget - Free SEO research tool ...	⊞ Edit	Remove
☑ Keyword Suggestions for Google - SEO Tools - Keyword Su...	⊞ Edit	Remove
☐ Craigslist Seeker - Search the 'for sale' section of craigslist....	⊞ Edit	Remove
☐ I'm Feeling Lucky - Search and navigate to the best result	⊞ Edit	
☐ Search Site - Search only on the current Web site	⊞ Edit	
☐ USA - Find pages in a country	⊞ Edit	
☐ Google Images - Search the Web for images	⊞ Edit	
☐ Google Video - Browse or search for video	⊞ Edit	

Figure 11.3

To add SEO plug-ins and search Google for additional SEO tools, select the "Add more buttons..." link at the top right of the screen. You must first download and install the plug-ins which are accessible by clicking on their associate buttons on the Google Toolbar. They will install into your web browser without any coding from you. Most SEO plug-ins are designed to work with the Internet Explorer, Google Chrome, and the Firefox browsers. You will find that you get the most functionality using the Firefox browser; it usually becomes the browser of choice for most people in charge of SEO.

> **NOTE:** *If you use Chrome, you'll find that many of the plug-ins available are not compatible. You can go to go to a web site called ChromePlugIns.org to find many of the SEO tools that are compatible with the Google Chrome browser.*

Choosing Plug-Ins Wisely

There are hundreds of SEO plug-ins that are available. Few plug-ins monitor more than one element of optimization, so in order to have multiple facets of your SEO strategy measured, you need multiple plug-ins. The key is determining what you need.

This is where I will put a big warning!

DO NOT BUY ANYTHING OR SIGN UP TO GET A FUNCTIONAL GOOGLE TOOLBAR PLUG-IN! DON'T GIVE A CREDIT CARD, AUTHORIZE A PAYPAL TRANSACTION OR GIVE BANK ACCOUNT INFORMATION TO ANYONE EITHER!

In texting, when you use capital letters you are yelling. And in a sense I was. Many of the plug-ins on Google are placed by people wanting to sell you their version of a plug-in. Most of the times it is just a modified version of a free one already available.

For web sites, you can choose among several different plug-ins, each usually monitoring something different. Some monitor links, while others monitor PageRank or keyword density, and still others monitor several elements. The selection process, then, begins with understanding what's available and what you can do with it.

So we have now hit the "Add more buttons…" link under Custom Tools on the "Adjust Toolbar Options" on the Google Toolbar. "So what do I do now?" you may be asking. Well, that's easy. In the search box, simply type "SEO" or "SEM" and press enter. You will see a list such as those in figure 11.4.

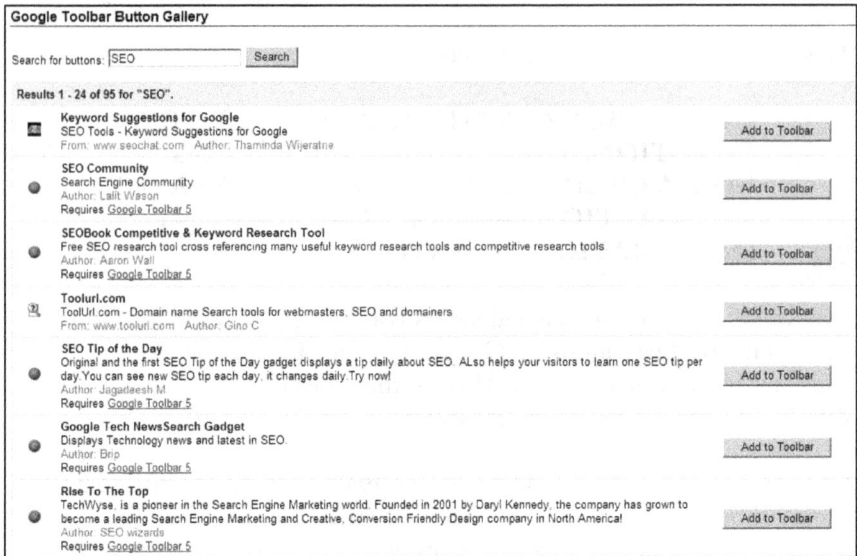

Figure 11.4

That search turns over 90 different SEO related buttons that you can add
to the Google Toolbar. I recommend the following for good SEO
Analysis:

1. Keyword Suggestions for Google
2. SEOBook Competitive and Keyword Research Tool
3. Google AdWords Campaign
4. SEO News
5. SEO Search Engine
6. Toolurl.com
7. Multiple Datacenter Link Popularity Check
8. SEO Tip of the Day
9. SEOBook Link Research Tool
10. SEOLens
11. Page Rank Check Monitor
12. Web site Traffic
13. Code to Text Ratio
14. Page Size Lookup

As you can see from this list, there are a variety of different tools that you
can plug into the Google toolbar. Everything from keyword research tools
to SEO news and blogs is available. All you have to do is decide which
ones are most useful for you and your SEO needs.

Each one has its own set of instructions but for the most part they ask you just to enter very little information such as a URL, IP Address, or keyword to get results.

Now let's take a look at the Alexa Toolbar and how that can help us in our quest to get better rankings.

Alexa Toolbar

The Alexa Toolbar, shown in figure 11.5, is tied into Alexa's web-traffic statistics, so the numbers that you'll find when you use this toolbar are a little skewed.

Figure 11.5

However, Alexa provides enough information to make the toolbar useful. Also, Alexa's results are a major influence on rankings found on the major search engines.

As you can see, the Alexa Toolbar looks quite a bit different from the Google Toolbar, and offers some good information. Once installed it also tracks where you go on the internet which helps Alexa determine the average traffic to a site. So visiting your own web sites frequently will help to improve the rankings on a Alexa.

Installing the Alexa Toolbar

To install the Alexa Toolbar, type http://www.alexa.com/toolbar into your browser, as shown in figure 11.6.

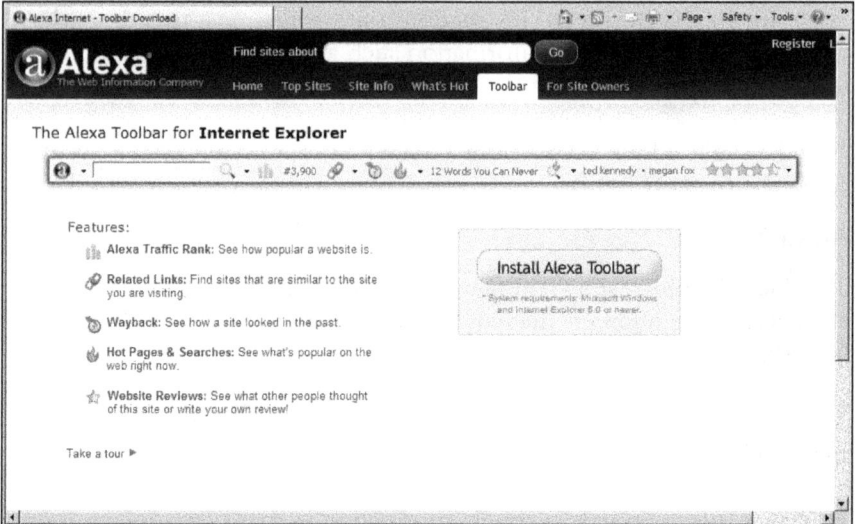

Figure 11.6

Once you click the "Install Alexa Toolbar" button, it will allow you to download and run the installation. Once that is completed you will be asked to give Alexa some demographic information, as shown in figure 11.7.

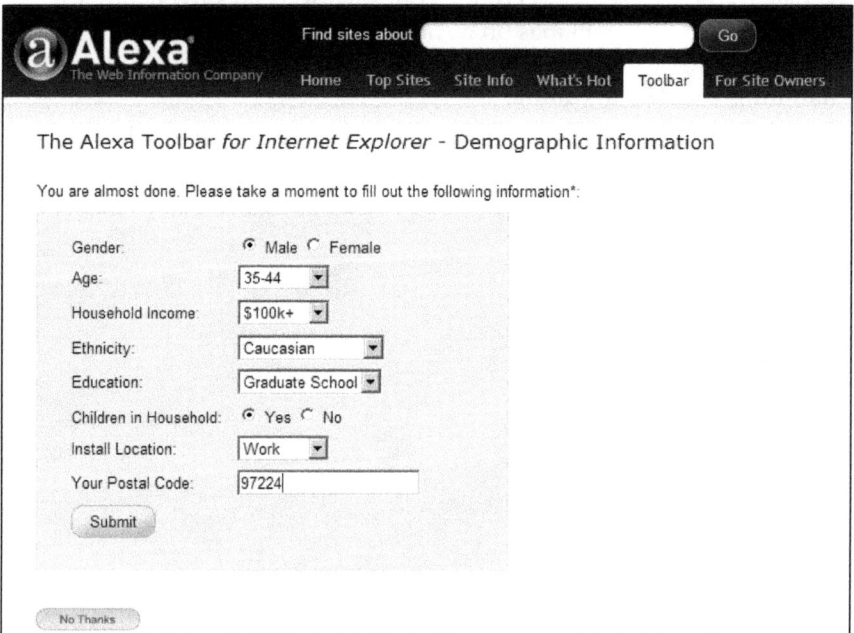

Figure 11.7

After you are done entering the demographic information and pressing "Submit," you will get a success message, as shown in figure 11.8.

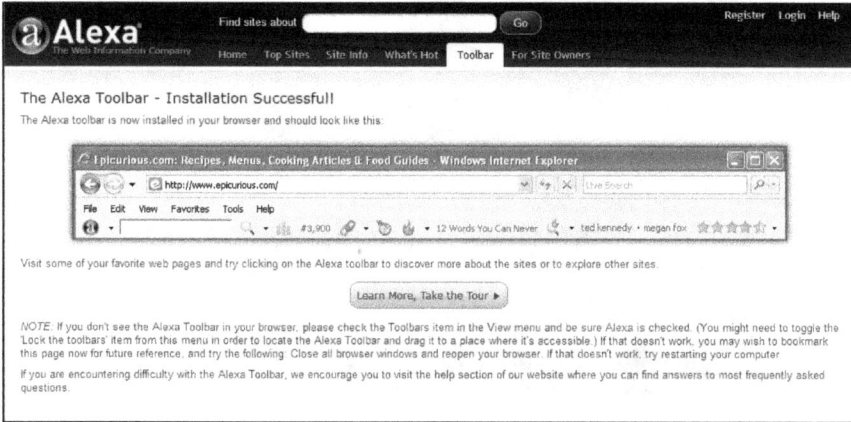

Figure 11.8

You will now be given an option to take the tour that explains all the features of the Alexa Toolbar, as shown in figure 11.9.

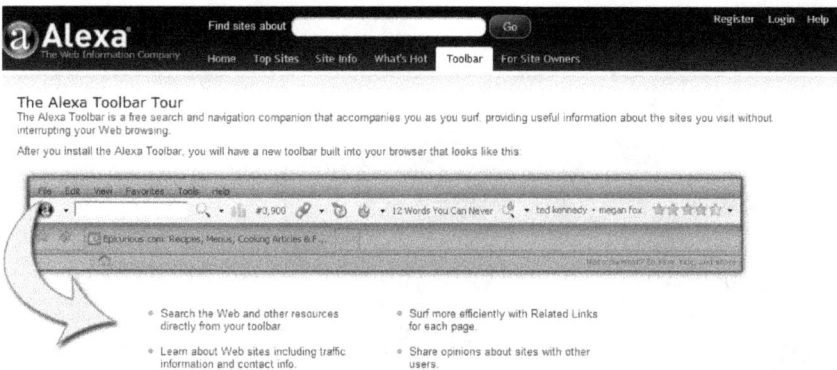

Web Search
The Alexa Web Search is a whole new way to search the web. Begin by typing your search term into the box then press enter. You will be transported to a world of behind-the-scenes information about each site on the web. Don't waste time sifting through lousy sites. Use the Alexa Web Search and know before you go.

Site Info
Alexa's exclusive Site Information allows you to peer behind the scenes of each site on the web. Get access to contact information, site stats and user reviews of web sites. Plus you can even write your own reviews.

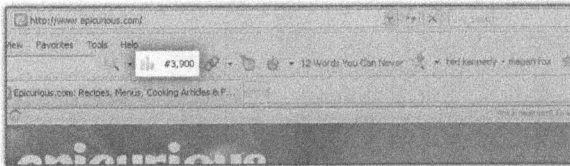

Related Links
Alexa's Related Links are a great way to discover new sites. As you surf the web, the toolbar is constantly updating with information about where other users visit.

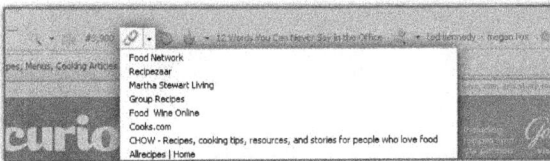

The Wayback Machine
Having trouble getting access to your favorite site or want to see what it looked like in the past? The Wayback Machine can transport you back in time to see archived copies of your favorite sites. Click the Wayback button, select a date, and go!

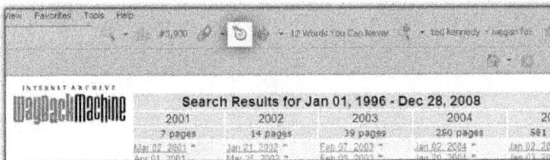

Figure 11.9

Analytics

Analytics are used to determine all kinds of things about the traffic to your web site. There are many packages that can cost stacks of money, but most do not track or report half as well as Google Analytics. The sales techniques used by those companies to sell their inferior software are interesting and usually pretty much the same and don't compare to Google Analytics. I recommend using Google Analytics. You can always look for better products but watch out if these are their only claims:

A. "Install on your own server"
B. "Restore historical data from files"
C. "Can track behind a firewall"
D. "Track robots, crawlers, and spiders"

Google Analytics is a free web site statistics application that you can use to track your web site traffic. You can begin using Google Analytics by going to www.google.com/analytics. You must have a Google user name to access the program.

If you do not have a Google user name, you can create one when you sign in the first time by provide an e-mail address and a password. Type the verification word from the graphic provided, and then agree to the Terms of Service by clicking "I accept. Create my account."

Once you've created your user name and password, accessing the tracking capabilities of Google is easy. You'll need to copy a small piece of code that Google gives you onto your web site pages just before the closing Body tag: "<\Body>". Let's take a look at the text that Google provides for the coding of your web site (Figure 11.10). After you've added the code to your web site, it will take a few days for Google to gather enough information to provide reports about it. More useful information will come after a full month of analytics.

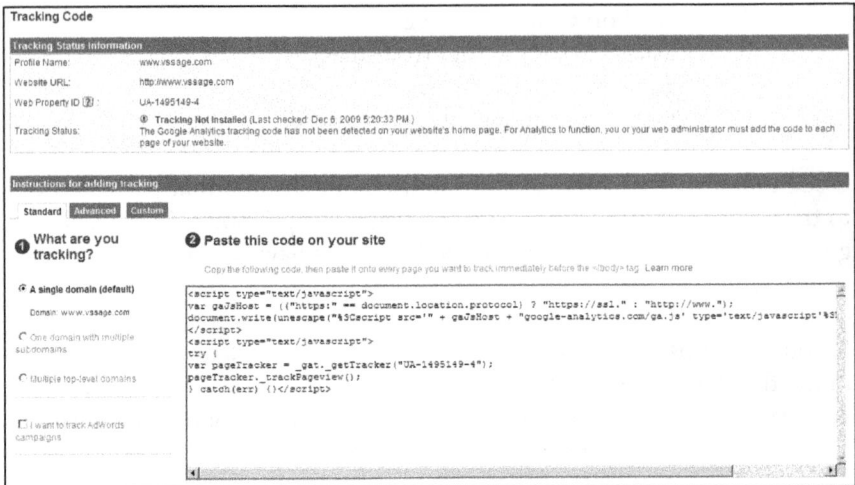

Figure 11.10

Google Analytics is a service provided by Google that allows you to view and interact with detailed statistical information about the visitors to your web site. After you have given Google some time to collect information about the visitors to your web site, you can formulate that into reports.

The information from Google Analytics allows you to see who is visiting your web site, how they are getting there, how long they stayed, what browser the visitors used, what keywords were used, and most importantly, what the visitors did once they were on your web site.

Being able to quickly access relevant information about your web site visitors is important because it will allow you address a range of marketing issues, relating both to your web site and your business as a whole. You will be able to track online and offline marketing campaigns, understand what your customers and prospective customers are looking for, and pinpoint areas of your web site that need improvement.

When you first login to Google Analytics and select the domain you want to view, if you have more than one, you are presented with a Dashboard view of your domain, such as the one showing LocalNewsDay.com (Figure 11.11).

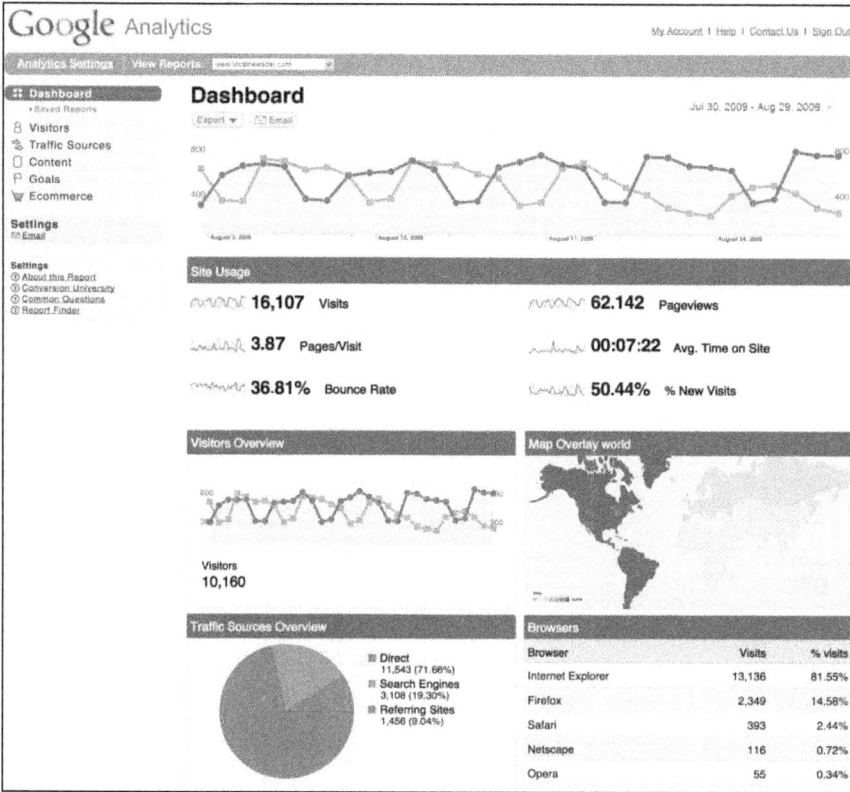

Figure 11.11

Most web site owners could only wish for over 16,000 visits in a single month such as those pictured here from the monthly report for LocalNewsDay.com. However, there is a story here. When I took over their web site's optimization two years ago, the monthly visits only averaged about 800-900. It is absolutely amazing what being at the top of Google and Bing for your keyword searches can do. This is why you need SEO for your web site.

Notice a search on "Orlando alternative news" on Bing or Google places LocalNewsDay.com on the first page of every major search engine, as shown in figure 11.12. Understanding and utilizing relevant analytics about your web site visitors will allow you to make your web site work harder for you, increase your ROI, increase your search engine rankings, generate more sales leads and allow you to better allocate resources.

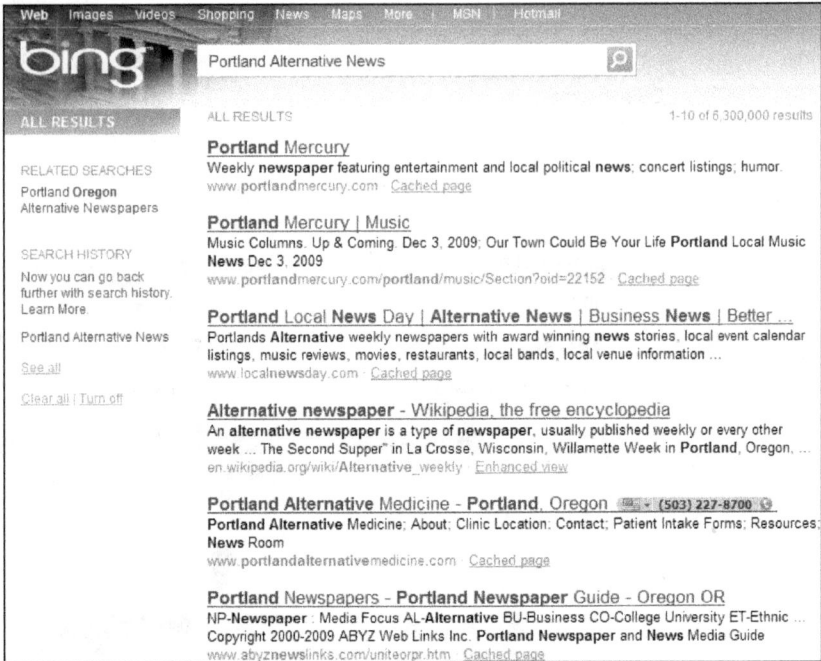

Figure 11.12

Now let's take a look at some of the reports and information you can obtain from Google Analytics to help you.

Analysis in Action

Access to visitors' statistics is one thing, but the true value of analytics comes in the form of analysis and action. Improvements to your web site should come out of a defined process and a decision based on information and knowledge. Analytics allows you to make those decisions and then measure the results. Below is a list of some of the most informational analyses from Google Analytics:

- Visitors
- Traffic Sources
- Intelligence Reports
- Expanded Goals
- Site Engagement Goals
- Advanced Table Filtering
- Expanded Mobile Reporting
- Share Advanced Segments

- Share Custom Reports
- Multiple Custom Variables

Google Analytics gives you many technical graphs, but value is only gained when that data is used to drive action to improve your web site. So how do we begin to analyze results in Google Analytics?

Firstly, you need to understand what your web site is about and what it actually does for your business. This may seem like a obvious place to start, and hopefully you know this by now.

So what is the purpose of your web site? Is it to generate leads? To sell products or services? To register subscribers? To provide support? Once you identify the purpose of your web site you can begin to identify ways to improve your web site. Generally your initial focus will either be content or a specific process you want to optimize.

The most important ways to improve your web site content is by analyzing Google Analytics reports in the next section.

Analyzing the Keywords Report
The first report after viewing how many visitors you received should be the keywords information under Traffic Sources as shown in Figures 11.13a and 11.13b. Do the keywords align with the purpose of your site or business? Are there keywords that are not optimized but are drawing relevant visitors?

If you identify an organic keyword that is important to your business, but has a high bounce rate, then develop content that specifically targets visitors using that keyword.

All traffic sources sent a total of 852 visits

20.07% Direct Traffic	Search Engines 459.00 (53.87%)
26.06% Referring Sites	Referring Sites 222.00 (26.06%)
53.87% Search Engines	Direct Traffic 171.00 (20.07%)

Top Traffic Sources

Sources	Visits	% visits	Keywords	Visits	% visits
google (organic)	330	38.73%	weldsafe	23	5.01%
(direct) ((none))	171	20.07%	discount welding supplies	21	4.56%
quimbycorp.com (referral)	121	14.20%	weldsafe.com	21	4.68%
bing (organic)	60	7.04%	welding supplies portland oregon	12	2.61%
yahoo (organic)	53	6.22%	bsx welding jacket	11	2.40%
view full report			view full report		

Figure 11.13a

Figure 11.13b

Analyzing the Site Search Report

Setup Site Search as shown in Figure 11.14 to identify gaps in content. Are people searching for something that your site already answers? If so, you should look at your navigation system. Can they get there easily?

If Site Search contains search terms that you know won't bring up relevant content on your site, you need to ask yourself why. Do these search terms identify opportunities to generate new content or fill the desires of your web site visitors?

Figure 11.14

Analyze the Top Content Report

When you look at top content report are there any pages that have a low average time on page or a high bounce rate? This generally indicates that a page isn't giving visitors what they are seeking. Review the pages that have the lowest time on page and highest bounce rate.

Figure 11.15

Sidebar: What is the bounce rate as shown in Figure 11.15?

Google Analytics can tell you how many of your visitors are *bouncing* from your site. This is labeled as your "bounce rate," which is the percentage of visitors coming to your site and leaving immediately.

High percentages of bounces is an indication that your site is not optimized properly, or visitors are not finding what they want based on their keyword searches.

This is a big problem, especially if the bounces happen on landing pages that are designed to greet visitors, contain a lot of information, or are for marketing URLs. Visitors who bounce from your site are not finding what they thought they would find, based on the search engine results or advertisements they clicked through.

You can begin to see how to analyze results in Google Analytics based on the purpose of your web site. Once you understand how your site works as a business tool, you can use Google Analytics to inform your process.

Google Analytics With Intelligence Reports

How would you like to have 24-hour a day access to a dedicated assistant who is focused exclusively on your site's analytics? Your assistant would be so diligent and detailed that they wouldn't miss a thing. Sound too good to be true? We're giving you one. Say "Hello" to Analytics Intelligence.

Your new hardworking assistant, Analytics Intelligence, can't replace you or a professional analyst. It can, however, find key information for you and your professional analysts so that your team can focus on making strategic decisions, instead of sifting through an endless sea of data.

Analytics Intelligence constantly monitors your web site's traffic. Anytime something significant happens, it adds an automatic alert in your Intelligence reports. If your bounce rate suddenly jumps on one of your referrals, Analytics Intelligence creates an alert. Of course, it's up to you to go find out that the bounce rate jumped because someone inadvertently changed the landing page or for some other reason. But you might not have noticed that there was a problem that needed fixing if your trusty assistant hadn't alerted you. Figures 11.16 and 11.17 show the alerts screen in Analytics Intelligence.

Figure 11.16

Figure 11.17

The automatic alerts will give a webmaster immediate information about traffic jumps or changes according to the configured thresholds you create. This can include major traffic changes to certain pages on the web site, a change in a page's bounce rate, page views, or a higher or lower than usual visitor stream from a specific country, state or region as shown in the automatic alerts in Figure 11.17.

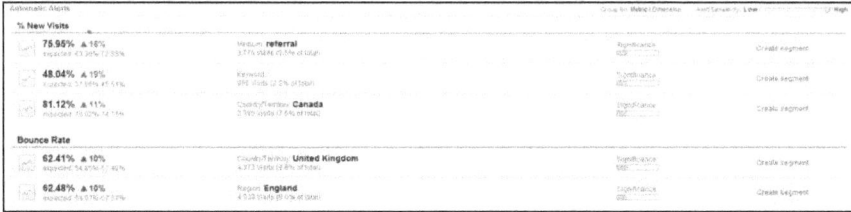

Figure 11.17

This gives the webmaster a quick overview of traffic developments on a specific web project or web site.

There are built in alerts that you can choose, but you can take Intelligence reports to the next level with Custom Alerts. These allow you to define your own alert triggers and receive an email alert. For example you can create a Custom Alert to notify you when your Google AdWords campaign traffic meets a revenue target or when your organic keyword terms from your SEO efforts has resulted in a certain number of visitors to your site.

There is almost a limitless number of alerts you can configure. Now it's time to set some goals in Google Analytics in the next section.

New Feature of Google Analytics Goals

A web site goal is a high value action that you would like your web site visitors to perform. On a content or lead generation site, this could include subscribing to an email newsletter or completing a contact form. On an e-commerce site this could be the completion of a checkout process. You can access goal data across numerous reports within Google Analytics, plus you will have access to goal specific reports under the 'Goals' tab.

If you have ever set up optimization or visitor goals in Google Analytics, one feature that you may have wanted is the ability to set more than four goals per profile. Now, Google Analytics profile can be setup with 20 goals. These are also now conveniently arranged in four groups containing five goals each.

Another new feature is the addition of site engagement goals. Standard goals are great for reporting on particular actions you want your visitors to take (buying online, filling out a contact form or registering for your email newsletter), but what if your primary objective is providing quality content and an engaging experience for your visitors?

Site engagement goals is your answer. Now you can set a goal conversion for time on site or pages per visit allowing you to access the power of goal reports within Google Analytics. If you are a SMB (Small to Medium Business), non-profit, government, or any organization with a content- or branding-focused site you should definitely begin using site engagement goals.

Mobile Reporting in Google Analytics

Google Analytics now allows for improved tracking of mobile devices, so you can now track interactions within your iPhone and Android apps to measure usage and engagement.

A new tracking code for mobile sites built using PHP, Perl, JSP and ASPX will also become available, allowing you to track all web-enabled mobile devices (not just mobile devices that run JavaScript).

Tips to Help You Utilize Google Analytics

1. Setup e-commerce tracking. If you have an e-commerce web site make sure you enable e-commerce tracking within your Google Analytics web site profile and add appropriate e-commerce tags to your web site. If you don't have an e-commerce web site you can still use e-commerce reports to associate a dollar value to particular web site visitors.

2. Link your Google AdWords account to your Google Analytics account. Once your accounts are linked you will have access to AdWords visitor data within Google Analytics.

3. Track your marketing campaigns. Campaign tracking is a crucial element in understanding how your marketing campaigns are performing. By tagging online and offline campaigns you can begin to evaluate and compare the effectiveness of your marketing initiatives. Tag everything!

4. Manually tag your CPC (Cost Per Click) campaigns. If you use a CPC system other than Google AdWords, you will need to manually tag your campaign URLs. CPC campaigns that are not tagged will be logged as "organic" (or unpaid) searches within Google Analytics.

Chapter 12 – What Not to Do

I have so many instances and references where I myself have made mistakes or where others have fallen before me and I have learned from their mistakes. In this chapter we will talk about:

- Abnormal Keyword Placement
- SEO Spam
- Doorway Pages
- Meta Jacking
- Page Cloaking
- IP Delivery/Page Cloaking
- Link Farms
- Spamblogs
- Page Highjacking
- Sybil Attacks
- Link Bombing
- What to Do If You Have Been Banned
- Problem Pages and Work-Arounds
- Validating Your HTML

Abnormal Keyword Delivery

The reason I am discussing this first is because it is the most common occurrence. I read all the time on SEO blogs that a person got his web site on the first page of Google by placing his keywords a hundred times at the bottom of his web site landing page in text that was the same color as the background of his web site. The person is so excited that he discounts and ignores all the professionals who comment that he shouldn't do this. Sometime the blog creator or commenter who has his site on the first page of Google even bad mouths the SEO professionals trying to help him.

I come back and read all the time how just a few short months later, the same guy that was so excited that his web site was on the first page of Google has written, "You guys were right. Google banned my URL for doing this." It is easy to temporarily be the most relevant site on Google the wrong way. But Google and the other major search engines have ways of figuring it out quite quickly. And once you are banned, you better call in the pros to help you. There is a section dedicated to this as the end of this chapter.

SEO Spam

SEO spam is the SEO version of email spam. Email spam pops up in your inbox where it's least wanted and those who are sending it believe that the law of averages is on their side. They think if you send out enough messages, eventually someone will respond.

SEO spam uses the same principle, except SEO spam fills the search engine results pages on search engines with results that have little or no value to the searcher. This can get you quickly banned. Imagine if you went to Google and every time you did a search you got results that were for something totally different than you searched for, or if the top 10 spaces of the search results were filled with the same company. If that happened you would switch to Bing in a heartbeat to get better results. Right?

Google and the other major search engines don't want this to happen. So if you do something that a search engine sees as spamming, your search rankings will be penalized. It's now even more likely that you'll be removed from search rankings entirely. If Google bans your URL it's as if you web site has been removed from the internet. It is almost invisible.

A term for some SEO spam is called *black hat SEO*. Black hat SEO refers to the use of aggressive SEO strategies, techniques and tactics that focus only on search engines and not a human audience. Some examples of black hat SEO techniques include keyword stuffing, link farms, invisible web site text and doorway pages, which we will learn about later in this chapter.

Black Hat SEO is more frequently used by those who are looking for a quick financial return rather than a long-term investment on their web site.

> **NOTE:** *Black Hat SEO will most likely result in your URL being banned from major search engines. However, since the focus is usually on quick high return business models, most experts who use Black Hat SEO tactics consider being banned from search engines a somewhat irrelevant risk. Black Hat SEO may also be referred to as Unethical SEO or just spamdexing.*

To make things a little more perplexing, search engines change their definitions of spam regularly. What works and is acceptable today may well be classified as spam tomorrow. This can have a profound effect on your rankings. One day you may be ranked high and on page one of a search and the next you may find that you're on page 8 of the results all because of the links you maintain.

The easiest way to monitor search engine changes is to keep up with what's happening in SEO on the Google Webmaster Central Blog (http://googlewebmastercentral.blogspot.com/). You can also learn about what's changing on ISEdb–Internet Search Engine Database (www.isedb.com), High Rankings Advisor (www.highrankings.com), and SEONews.com.

The general rule is, if you're doing something on your web site that you have to worry might get you banned from major search engines, you probably shouldn't be doing it.

If you read anywhere that SEO spam techniques are okay, or that you won't get caught because search engines don't pay attention, ignore this advice at all costs. The penalties differ according to the search engine, but if you are caught spamming even once, most search engines will delist you from search results immediately. I have seen it a hundred times and have had it happen to me on accident when I went overboard experimenting. Yes, even the experts make a mistake or two. But we learn from them.

Here's what is definitely considered spam:

- Trying to make your site appear more relevant to the search engines by embedding hidden keywords in your web site.
- Artificially generating links to your web site from unrelated sites for the purpose of increasing your ranking based on link analysis.
- Artificially generating traffic to your web site so that it appears more popular than it really is.
- Submitting your web site repeatedly for inclusion in the rankings.

   NOTE: *You should submit your site once and then wait at least six weeks before submitting it again.*

Doorway Pages

Doorway pages are created to do well for particular phrases. They are also known as portal pages, jump pages, bridges, gateway pages, entry pages, and by other names as well. Search engines have developed ways to easily identify these pages. They are primarily to make a page seem more relevant for search engines, and not for human beings.

You should always have your pages designed for human eyes and not just for a search engine. There are various ways to deliver doorway pages. The low-tech way is to create and submit a web page that is targeted toward a particular phrase or keyword.

These pages tend to be very generic. It's easy for people to copy them, make minor changes, and submit the revised page. Sometimes these are so similar that the search consider these duplicates and automatically exclude them from their listings.

Another problem is that users sometimes arrive at the doorway page. Say a real person searched for "welding supplies" and the doorway page appears. They click through, but that page probably lacks any detail about the welding supplies that you sell. To get them to that content, webmasters usually propel visitors forward with a prominent "Click Here" link or with an automatic page redirect.

Some search engines no longer accept pages using any redirects (sometimes referred to as fast Meta refresh). This has led to some black hatters doing a bait-and-switch, or "code-swapping," on the search engines. Some black hat webmasters submit a real web page, wait for it to be indexed and then swap it with a doorway page.

The trouble is that a search engine may revisit at any time figure out what you have done.

Meta Jacking

Meta jacking is the taking of the Meta tagging from one page and placing them on another page hoping to obtain good rankings and relevance. However, simply taking Meta tags from a page will not guarantee a page will do well. In fact, sometimes resubmitting the exact page from another location does not gain the same position as the original page.

Agent Delivery

When you target a single doorway page to a single search engine this is called "agent delivery." Each search engine reports an "agent" name, just as each browser reports a name.

Agent delivery pages are tailored pages that direct users to the actual content you want them to see. It also has the added benefit of "cloaking" your code from only the search engine you are targeting. The major search engines have gotten wise to this, though. They change the name they report specifically to help keep people honest.

IP Delivery / Page Cloaking

To avoid the agent name changing, you can also deliver pages to the search engines by allowing only the search engines IP address. This means if a bot, crawler, or spider visits your doorway page and reports an IP address that matches the search engine's or the IP resolves to a certain host name, it can see the code of your web site.

Link Farms

Link farms are simply pages of links that are created just to artificially boost a linking strategy in an effort to speed the appearance of the web site in the top search ranking positions. Typically you pay money to join them or buy software that allows you to mass send your links.

Spamblogs

These are software or machine-generated blogs which have only one purpose – increase search engine rankings.

Page Highjacking

Page hijacking occurs when very popular webpage coding is stolen and used to represent your web site to the search engines. When users perform a search and see your webpage in the search results, they click through the link only to be taken to your actual page.

Sybil Attacks

Sybil attacks are when a spammer creates multiple web sites that are all interlinked for the purpose of creating a false link structure. These are sometimes called incestuous links.

Link Bombing

One anchor text tactic to avoid is link bombing . Link bombing refers to the methods used by black hat SEOs to artificially inflate their web site ranking by connecting an unrelated keyword to a specific web site. For link bombing to work, more than one web site designer must be willing to participate in a link exchange.

What to Do If You Have Been Banned

If you have been banned from the major search engines, you may find it the worst experience of your life, especially since the internet is now the official yellow pages for most and being banned from the major search engines is like locking your business doors and taking the phone off the hook.

Most of the time you will know what was done that got you banned. In this case, it may require explaining to the search engine the tactic you employed, why you employed it, and how you fixed it. Google, for instance, allows you to send in an explanation by going to the Google Webmaster Tools (https://www.google.com/webmasters/tools) and clicking on the "Site Reconsideration" link on the left-hand side. This will take you to the web page which outlines written and video instructions to resubmit your web site.

It could take a couple of months to a year to be reindexed into the search engine. In some cases it is quicker and easier to ditch the old URL and start a brand new one. Then you have to work your way back to the top of the rankings again. Just make sure that you have fixed or stopped doing whatever was done to get your URL banned in the first place.

Chapter 13 – Marketing Principles

Throughout my career I have been thought of by many as being one of the best sales persons both online and in real life. There are many things that help me make sales. In this chapter, I will outline the little things that add up one by one to help you make sales. Although the focus here is on online sales, these are sales principles that you should use every day both online and in real life to help you sell.

Sales Principles You Should Adopt

These are my top 12 direct marketing principles you can use to make sure your internet marketing really works for you:

Stability

People want to know you are not going to disappear overnight so if you've been in business for any length of time, this will add credibility to you and your offers.

Statistics

Use genuine statistics to give you more credibility when listing the number of customers served, money saved, profits made, true results, and so on.

Testimonials

I can't overestimate the importance of getting relevant and credible reviews from your customers and clients, saying how you and your products or services have helped them.

Self Credibility

If you can, establish yourself as an expert in your field. Not everyone can write numerous books or be on TV. However, you can write articles and have them published on your product, service, or industry. You can run workshops that are designed to demonstrate or train how to use your products or how effective your services are.

Reprints of articles about you in the press or having your articles published in the media lend weight to your credibility as the expert or authority in your market and are highly valuable to you. Show your market that you are in demand, and have status as an expert.

You can also show you're an expert with industry certifications, awards, memberships, and accomplishments that are relevant to your market.

Demonstrations

It's a lot cheaper to sell online with the use of online videos or 'how to' DVDs to sell your product. If you hire a sales person he can only be one place at a time. The internet can be the equivalent of hundreds of sales people. A web site that is properly designed can make it very easy to show a demonstration of your product or services, both on and offline.

You can also create and distribute a demonstration eBook by printing it out and talking through what it contains live on screen. Camtasia is free software that lets you make a screen capture video where you can demonstrate your web site talking though the sales letter or giving a demo of how easy it is to download your eBook.

> **NOTE:** *You can also print eBooks cost effectively at Lulu.com and CreateSpace.com.*

Guarantee

If you can't guarantee the product or service you're selling, then find something else to sell that you can guarantee. To really make your potential customers feel safe buying from you, have an ironclad guarantee.

Accessibility

On your web site, having your full contact detail information is a big boost to your potential customer confidence. Using just an email contact or a form shows you are hiding. Put your email, phone, and address that shows that you are in the U.S. and help your websites crediblity.

> **NOTE:** *Never give a P.O. Box as your address as it immediately makes people suspicious.*

The Personal Touch

Be visible in the business you're in and make sure you have a live voice answer your phone if possible. In my SEO business, if I let voicemail pickup for one day I never get a sale. If I answer the phone, I usually always make a sale. Also, tell your customers about yourself. Make it personal to them and show them you are a real individual.

Admit Imperfections Upfront

No matter how good your product or service is, it will most likely have a disadvantage somewhere. Admit it up front and honestly comment on this fact.

Answer questions and objections in a timely manner when a potential customer asks them via email or the phone. Buyers buy more often when they can call an office throughout the week and email at any time with questions and get a human response.

People Will Buy to Save Money

People who are interested in your product or service will usually do nothing unless you ask for the sale and give them incentive. People are just bombarded by too many sales pitches and try to choose the best one. The best pitch is to create urgency to buy now, such as informing them that the price is going up next week. But you have plenty of options here: you can offer a reduced price, a bundled special deal on your products or services, or a smaller free item for buying an larger item now.

Special Tactic for Creating Urgency

A special tactic to create urgency is to put an end date on your promotions and discounts – buy it now before the price goes up next week, next month, tomorrow. Even if your regular price is your promotional price, do a monthly campaign. When they look online they see a higher price if you don't buy by the end of the month.

If your business looks like it is always in permanent sale mode, there's no urgency for the customer to buy. Customers are not stupid; they see the advertising and know that this company ALWAYS has a sale on.

That's why it's important you create a deadline for your promotion. By having a defined end date showing in bold letters, it creates urgency and a reason for your potential customer to act now or lose out on saving money.

Tell People the Value They Are Getting

The discounts and value to the customer are not always obvious. So make it clear. If you put a value next to the items you are selling, don't assume your prospect or customer has worked it out for themselves. If the total value is $250, tell them it is $250 because if you leave them to add it up for themselves they generally won't do it.

Research

Research is an essential aspect of marketing. Inadequate research of your products and target market is one of the biggest pitfalls that can affect a marketing strategy. Research provides a wealth of information that is vital to your sales.

Determine what market is going to most likely benefit from the product or service you provide. This is the group of individuals you will want to target – in some areas, there may be multiple groups. While it may be possible to market to all these groups, in most situations it is better to market to a single group which contain a large percentage of similar traits. This makes it easier to consolidate a marketing plan as well as eliminate a significant amount of research, time, and effort.

The second aspect which needs to be researched for a marketing plan to be successful is to research your competition. It is also one of the reasons why marketing fails to produce appropriate results. Researching your competition is not just about researching the prices of a competitor. It includes noting things such as their sales techniques, finding out what marketing tools, keywords, and resources they use.

Many business owners and beginning internet marketers fail to note anything more than price and perhaps general layout of their competitors web site and end their research there. They miss vital information that can save time, money, and effort when it comes to setting up their own marketing strategy. If you are not the most successfully-marketed business on the internet promoting your product or service, find out who is. Find out how they market and what makes them successful.

Collect information on the types of deals, offers, discounts and promotions that your competition uses and offer something different to help your business stand out. Many people simply do what their competition does. In doing so, they often lower their marketability and their marketing plan can ultimately fail in this area. You might pick up more market share by doing what the completion doesn't.

Marketing Tools

Having enough research to create your marketing plan is only the first step in solving the problems that often cause marketing plans to fail. The next step is to take the time to pick out the right tools. Having the right tools for the job is essential to ensuring you get the most out of your marketing strategies.

Marketing tools have diversified over the years. Tools are not limited strictly to email and promotional options. Video, social networking, SMS texting, Blogs, Twitter, Facebook, PPC, and many more are available to you. You just have to pick the tools that are going to be easy for you to learn, use, and require minimal maintenance with maximum potential results.

Don't Just Dream It, Do It!

One of the biggest reasons I am so successful is that if I get an idea, I do it. Nothing stands in my way. Hence you are reading this book because I came up with an idea for it while taking a shower. Don't picture that, by the way. In John Pinette's words, "You'll have nightmares!"

One of the biggest reasons why marketing strategies and businesess end up failing is lack of action and giving up. Marketing is an active part of your business, it is not a "set it in motion and let it run on its own" component of a web site. In order to ensure that a marketing strategy succeeds you must be actively engaged in working that plan and revisit it and make the strategy better based on experience. This means that email marketing messages should be updated and redesigned regularly.

SMS, Facebook, and Twitter messages should be rewritten after every send. These messages should be short, contain only the minimum necessary information, and focus on one item at a time. It is important to remember that this type of marketing is relatively new and involves sending messages to Wiki's, blogs, members, and mobile devices that often indicate repeat messages.

Videos should be produced, edited, and updated to as high a level as possible. Computers and technology can turn just about any computer into a production studio with the right software. Keep videos interesting, engaging, and relevant. The videos should be related to the company, the products, or the services offered.

It is important to set up a marketing schedule and find out how much time, generally through trial and error, that you need each day, week or month to handle all your marketing tasks and keep everything up to date.

The reasons why a marketing plan might fail are numerous. I hate to outline some of them here, but you need to know so you can take steps avoid them. Some of these reasons include the following: failing to do the proper research into the market, not doing proper SEO, not having the right tools available, not researching cheaper delivery methods, having too many tools or not using the tools you have effectively, and not having inventory on hand that you are selling.

Taking the time to make sure that you have the information you need as well as putting in the effort to ensure your success can go a long way to eliminating these reasons.

When you develop a marketing message, you have to hit many levels of desire. Good marketing happens when you give logical reasons for your prospect's emotional-buying decisions. Some good marketing messages include:

- Save time
- Save money
- Make money
- Try for free
- Avoid effort
- Increase happiness
- Find success
- Be pain-free
- Get better health
- Have fun
- Enjoy your life
- Gain praise
- Feel safe and secure
- Feel liked or loved
- Be popular

Your task is to find a message which matches to your product or service and start promoting your marketing message in your marketing strategy.

See What Your Potential Clients Desire and Play on That

You should develop the ability to see what others want, need, and desire through your own research. You will be successful if you are always satisfying your customer's needs. Sometimes you have to look for the gap and create a new product or service or develop an improvement of an existing product or service.

You should always focus on service and deliver what you promise on time. My general rule is to always under promise and over deliver. Tell a customer that he/she won't have it until Friday even though it arrives on Wednesday. If something is delayed, the customer is not upset and when you deliver it early you look like the hero.

The internet allows you to start small and grow to any size business that you want to. Following the advice and principles I have laid out in this chapter will help your customer numbers grow and your profits grow with them.

Dealing With Adversity

My last words of advice are always maintain honesty and integrity in your dealings and stay true to your values even when dealing with stressful situations. Every business owner is going to have to deal with anxiety, frustration and problems, so cope with them by developing tenacity and perseverance.

If sales don't happen the first time you talk to a potential client, look at these statistics from the National Sales Executive Association:

- 2% of sales are made on the 1st contact;
- 3% of sales are made on the 2nd contact;
- 5% of sales are made on the 3rd contact;
- 10% of sales are made on the 4th contact;
- 80% of sales are made on the 5th – 12th contact.

For most businesses, if you don't offer an opt-in contact, like a regular email newsletter or blog postings, you're missing out on most of your potential sales.

When setting up an opt-in internet marketing campaign, you should offer incentives to subscribe. To entice people to opt-in, you can offer:

- Special pricing for email list members
- A first look at new products
- Ability for customer to select subjects and emails they receive
- Promise not to share email or other personal info with other companies

Using opt-in contact allows you to significantly increase conversions by introducing yourself over time to your potential customers, in a soft-sell manner

Web site optimization is important; the goal is increased internet traffic, sales and sales leads. But whether you've hired an online SEO consultant or you're doing the process yourself, affordable search engine optimization by itself doesn't accomplish those last points which increase sales and sales leads. It just drives the potential customers to your web site. You still have to close the deal.

Chapter 14 – Having Multiple Landing Pages

Most web sites selling anything need to target more than three keywords. Even if you just sell a single product or service. So what do you do to promote your web site and focus on many keywords since many of the major search engines only allow a web page to be relevant for three keywords.

The answer is a simple one but the execution is about the most complex of any part of your web site's code. The answer is that you need to create a perfectly optimized landing page for every three keywords you want to focus on. You then have to have the search engines index all those additional pages separately as separate landing pages.

Now, here is the hard part. Google and the other major search engines require a site map to tell them the landing pages you want to index. Not just any, there is a standard called Sitemap protocol 0.90.

> **WARNINGS:** *There are so many web sites and web developers on the Internet that claim they can create a sitemap. Many just create pages with links and call them a sitemap. Also, there has been many updates to the Sitemap Protocol and many web sites still push older versions. I highly recommend that if you are not a professional developer you go to a trusted source such as SMMaker.com or SMCreator.com and have them professionally create and install a Sitemap for your web site.*

In this chapter I am going to tell you how to make a Sitemap specially formulated to Google and Bing. And then how to tell Google and Bing where to look for your site map. As you saw from the warning above, it is a lot of work to create a site map and test it to see if it is working. It is so much easier to just visit either one of these sites and pay less than $15.00 to have it created for you at either of these web sites:

http://www.SMMaker.com
http://www.SMCreator.com

So let's take a look at how to create a site map.

Sitemaps XML format

Informing search engine crawlers This document describes the XML schema for the Sitemap protocol. The Sitemap protocol format consists of XML tags. All data values in a Sitemap must be entity-escaped. The file itself must be UTF-8 encoded.

The Sitemap must include the following:

- Begin with an opening <urlset> tag and end with a closing </urlset> tag.

- Specify the namespace (protocol standard) within the <urlset> tag.

- Include a <url> entry for each URL, as a parent XML tag.

- Include a <loc> child entry for each <url> parent tag.

All of the other tags are optional. Support for these optional tags may vary among search engines. Refer to each search engine's documentation for details.   For Google you must include this tag:

```
<urlset xmlns="http://www.sitemaps.org/schemas/sitemap/0.9">
```

Let's look at an example which shows a Sitemap that contains just a single URL:

```
<?xml version="1.0" encoding="UTF-8"?>
<urlset xmlns="http://www.sitemaps.org/schemas/sitemap/0.9">
  <url>
    <loc>http://www.Webseopros.com/</loc>
    <lastmod>2005-01-01</lastmod>
    <changefreq>monthly</changefreq>
    <priority>0.8</priority>
  </url>
</urlset>
```

All XML Tags

Here are all the tags that can be used in your site map and their syntaxes and descriptions.

\<urlset\> (required)

Encapsulates the file and references the current protocol standard.

\<url\> (required)

Parent tag for each URL entry. The remaining tags are children of this tag.

\<loc\> (required)

URL of the page. This URL must begin with the protocol (such as http) and end with a trailing slash, if your web server requires it. This value must be less than 2,048 characters.

\<lastmod\> (optional)

The date of last modification of the file. This date should be in W3C Date/time format. This format allows you to omit the time portion, if desired, and use YYYY-MM-DD.

\<changefreq\> (optional)

How frequently the page is likely to change. This value provides general information to search engines and may not correlate exactly to how often they crawl the page. Valid syntaxes are:
- always
- hourly
- daily
- weekly
- monthly
- yearly
- never

\<priority\> (optional)

The priority of this URL relative to other URLs on your site. Valid values range from 0.0 to 1.0. This value does not affect how your pages are compared to pages on other sites—it only lets the search engines know which pages you deem most important for the crawlers.

NOTE: *The default priority of a page is 0.5.*

The priority you assign to a page is not likely to influence the position of your URLs in a search engine's result pages. Search engines may use this information when selecting between URLs on the same site, so you can use this tag to increase the likelihood that your most important pages are present in a search index.

WARNING: *Assigning a high priority to all of the URLs on your site is not likely to help you. Since the priority is relative, it is only used to select between URLs on your site.*

Here is an example using the different tags:

```
<?xml version="1.0" encoding="UTF-8"?>
<urlset xmlns="http://www.sitemaps.org/schemas/sitemap/0.9">
<url>
<loc>http://www.webseopros.com</loc>
<lastmod>2010-05-20</lastmod>
<priority>0.5</priority>
</url>
<url>
<loc>http://www.webseopros.com/TA.php</loc>
<lastmod>2010-05-20</lastmod>
<priority>0.5</priority>
</url>
<url>
<loc>http://www.webseopros.com/SEO.php</loc>
<lastmod>2010-05-20</lastmod>
<priority>0.5</priority>
</url>
<url>
<loc>http://www.webseopros.com/SEM.php</loc>
<lastmod>2010-05-20</lastmod>
<priority>0.5</priority>
</url>
</urlset>
```

Saving your Site Map

Search engines know to look for a plain text site map at the root directory of your website where your Index page resides. It should be named "Sitemap.xml"

For instance it should be accessible using your site URL. If the Sitemap is located at http://www.webseopros.com/sitemap.xml and it can't include URLs from http://subdomain.Webseopros.com.

You can submit a sitemap using a port. If you submit a Sitemap using a path with a port number, you must include that port number as part of the path in each URL listed in the Sitemap file. For instance, if your

Sitemap is located at:

http://www.webseopros.com:100/sitemap.xml

then each URL listed in the Sitemap must begin with:

http://www.webseopros.com:100.

For more information from Google on the latest site map creating techniques visit this link:

http://www.google.com/support/webmasters/bin/topic.py?hl=en&topic=20986

Chapter 15 – Professional SEO Services

After reading this book you may have come to the conclusion that you don't want or have the time to invest in optimizing your web site. Or maybe you have investigated the competition and found that the amount of competition is too much for you to handle on your own. Whatever the reason, you may come to a point where you feel that hiring a professional is what you need to do.

I could just stop the chapter right here and say hey, e-mail me at:

Jason McCormick at Jason@WebSEOPros.com

My team and I will take care of you. If that is not what you want to do, let me give you some pointers to help you out. There are a lot of scam artists, cons, and the like which want to take the money from your bank account and do little or nothing in return. In fact I think it is easier to find the scam artists than the real thing.

If I were to guess on a ratio. There is probably 10 scammers for every 1 SEO consultant that knows enough to get you listed at the top of the search engines. The information in this chapter is crucial to learn to keep you from falling victim to scams.

Hiring the Right Professionals

In this business cutting corners is not an option, because the wrong SEO practices are far more detrimental to your site than doing nothing whatsoever. Virtually everyone of my major clients was first scammed by an SEO scammer before coming to me. In fact, it is not at all unusual to hear about a company or web site owner that's been scammed by a supposed SEO consultant who guaranteed them top placement in hundreds of search engines more than once.

One of the first clues is the absolute guarantee part. It's just not possible for anyone, even an SEO expert, to guarantee that your site will appear at number one of search engine rankings all the time. Nonetheless, many people claiming to be SEO experts will tell you they can do just that. Don't believe them.

In most cases, what happens is this: A web site designer or owner who has had to create a site for SEO decides he or she can implement SEO for others to make a profit. However, just because these people have done SEO on their own sites doesn't mean they can plan SEO and implement optimization techniques on your site in the most effective manner possible. Every site, company and industry have different optimization needs.

In most cases, it takes a team of people to perform proper SEO techniques for a business web site. That team might include someone to submit your site to directories and search engines, someone to create and submit articles to online resources, someone to design and implement SEO elements, someone to code the web site to make it attractive to search engines, and a project manager to manage the whole SEO program from beginning to end.

Recognizing SEO Scammers

There are certain things you should check or look for when choosing an SEO company. These are the following:

- Get references from them. See where their customers rank. Go one step further, though. If at the bottom of the referral web site's homepage it does not show that the SEO company you are checking out does their web design or SEO work, call the company and verify that their SEO work is handled by them.

- It is not uncommon for scammers to find a highly-ranked site and claim it is their work. In Website SEO Professional's case, most of our customers have let us place a link at the bottom of their homepage that states, "SEO Services Provided By: WebSEOPros.com" and a link to our page. It makes it easy for our customers to see we really do the work we say we do.

- Be wary if the prospective company says that they guarantee that your site will show up in the first page of results or even as the number one result every time! Time for a reality check: the algorithms that the search engines use are closely guarded trade secrets meaning that no one outside of a few people at the search engine companies knows exactly how it all works and they change regularly, especially for high competition keywords.

  Guaranteeing a certain page ranking is a sign of inexperience at best – and much more likely, indicates a scam.

- If you hear an obviously busy call center in the back ground, run. If their sales department is a room crowded with telemarketers trolling for business around the clock, it's a big red flag that you are being scammed.

- If they promise you 1,000+ visitors for one low price, you're probably paying them to post a fake job listing on Craigslist or Monster.com for an Administrative Assistant job that makes 80K a year and a link to your website. They'll get the traffic there alright. Not one of them will be interested in buying your product or service.

- They promise to secure you top rankings for keywords. Well usually they are right. They get you top rankings for long-tail keywords which are unlikely to be used by anyone.

  For starters, they're trying to sell you a guaranteed page ranking (but we know better, don't we?). If the keyword they're offering sounds a little fishy to you, look up its popularity with the free Google Keyword Tool we discussed in Chapter 1. See what its popularity is. Most likely there aren't many searches for that keyword or competition.

- Their services are offered at unrealistically low prices. There are some SEO scammers who lure victims by offering to optimize your site and run promotional campaigns for prices that sound entirely too good to be true. Usually they want the amount upfront and from a checking account rather than a credit card.

  An effective organic SEO campaign takes a significant amount of time and effort for keyword research, reworking page content, building high quality back links and designing and implementing traffic driving strategies. It's not something that can be done cheaply and definitely not all at once.

- RED FLAG: "We can give your web site an SEO tune up for $499.00."

- RED FLAG: "Results in 48 hours (or less). " If this could be done it would save everyone a lot of money and time. Everyone would be number one. Oh wait. They can't be. These scammers usually tell you that the results of optimizing a site aren't visible at all for at least a few weeks – and for the results to really begin trending in the right direction, you often need to wait up to six months. By then, they are gone and so is your money.

Again, do your due diligence. Look at their credentials, find out who's used their services in the past and what they have to say about the company. You should expect regular reports on how your keywords are performing and you should be able to easily get in touch by phone and speak to one of the SEO consultants to get their advice and input as needed. It needs to be an interactive process.

The best SEO companies have years of expertise in the field and know the most effective SEO methodologies inside and out. When algorithms change they also know how to determine the changes. Your placements on the major search engines may change from month to month but will return as your professional SEO company does what is necessary to get you back to the top.

What to Expect From Your SEO Company

When you find an SEO firm that offers the services that you need, you can expect to receive certain specific services from them. The services vary from firm to firm, but here's a list that you can use as a good rule of thumb:

- You should be provided with an initial professional SEO audit. The audit should thoroughly examine your sites URL properties, current SEO elements, problems with the current design and structure of your existing web site, keyword and competitor research. And include recommendations the recommended code changes.

- If you are trying to employ an SEO company that is a one man show who does the auditing, the optimization, the linking, the articles, the research, the social media, the web changes, monitors the analytics, the billing, and everything else, you will soon learn that no one can be an expert at everything and you will soon be lost amongst his many clients.

  The company you hire should employ a project manager who tracks all the needs of your company's web site and the reports. This person needs to be able to bring in the experts needed at the time they are needed and always be available by phone. If your SEO expert says he is only available by e-mail that is a red flag!

- You should be provided with recommendations for keywords and a plan to optimize your site. This report should indicate how each page of your web site is optimized including what on-page SEO elements such as HTML tags, keywords, and content needs to be changed on your web site on an ongoing basis.

- You should be provided with information on how the SEO company plans to perform the optimization of the internal site navigation. Your internal navigation can have a serious effect on how your site performs in search results, so a good SEO will examine and optimize that navigation structure.

- Your SEO company should be able to scan the Internet weekly for mentions of your domain name in Blogs and other social media and provide this in a weekly report. This is now known as "Reputation Management" and is a critical piece of any online presence. And should be part of your weekly SEO Report.

- Your SEO company should provide Grade A 3rd party website and SEO audits from AccuQuality.com or SEOAudits.com. They should run tests for accessibility, compliance, browser compatibility, usability, page errors, standards compliance on every page. Not just the homepage as the free ones do.

- The SEO company should be able to scan your web site weekly for design changes made that inadvertently broke links or strayed from the SEO goals set in place. These warnings should also be in your weekly SEO Report.

- A plan on how the SEO company intends to perform link building for your domain and verify they are only white hat techniques to sites relevant to your industry.

- The company you choose should have procedures and the ability to test the different search engine algorithms to detect changes. They should be able to immediately make changes to your web site to match those changes.

- A plan on how the SEO company will show their progress and the monitoring of your SEO efforts and keyword statistics. They should also be able to give you statistics on your major competitors as well. If the SEO company cannot provide you this information on a weekly basis, especially in the beginning, find another company.

- SEO requires ongoing efforts. The SEO company must be able to train your staff with the most successful methods for maintaining optimization and providing news articles and suggestions.

Professional SEO firms can offer a lot of benefits to your web site. After all, your core business is likely not SEO, but an SEO firm's is. The good ones can properly optimize your site, and your services, in less time than you can. For that reason alone, it should be enough to make you consider hiring an SEO firm, whether or not you end up doing so.

INDEX

www.ingramcontent.com/pod-product-compliance
Lightning Source LLC
Chambersburg PA
CBHW060006210326
41520CB00009B/836